CIDER
VINEGAR

CIDER VINEGAR

MAURICE HANSSEN

AN ARC BOOK

ARCO PUBLISHING COMPANY, INC.
219 Park Avenue South, New York, N.Y. 10003

An ARC Book
Published 1975 by Arco Publishing Company, Inc.
219 Park Avenue South, New York, N.Y. 10003
by arrangement with Thorsons Publishers Limited.

Library of Congress Catalog Card Number 74-27432
ISBN 0-668-03751-2

Printed in the United States of America

CONTENTS

FOREWORD

The merits of cider vinegar have been cele-
brated in print before now, but never — I
suspect — accompanied by the thorough research and scientific accuracy displayed by
Maurice Hanssen. To have done this in a
reasonably light-hearted way adds to the read-
ability.

Commencing with a detailed description of
manufacturing processes from the time of
autumn apple-picking, Maurice Hanssen continues with valuable information on the best
way to take cider vinegar therapeutically and
gives a detailed breakdown of the minerals,
organic matter and acetic acid found in this
most intriguing substance.

Cider vinegar is probably best known for its
slimming properties, and Maurice Hanssen
quotes chapter and verse for its success in this
direction, and this quality alone should create
very great interest. A natural substance really
does inspire confidence. But cider vinegar has
also been used with notable success in the
treatment of arthritis and rheumatism, insomnia, asthma, and heart conditions. These —
and other disorders — are all dealt with, and
clear instructions for the internal and external
application of cider vinegar are provided.

Like Maurice Hanssen, I believe in the importance of eating whole foods uncontaminated by chemical additives. Therefore I am delighted to find that his penultimate section is entitled 'Cider vinegar in the kitchen', and that it contains a host of appetizing recipes for salad dressings, sauces, chutneys, savoury dishes and drinks — all depending on the 'magic' ingredient of cider vinegar for their excellence. Dr. Johnson declared, 'He who does not mind his stomach will not mind much else', and I for one cannot imagine a better introduction to cider vinegar than that supplied in the culinary information you will find in this section.

That cider vinegar has a role to play in animal husbandry, I find very reassuring. We live in a world where animals are too often subjected to 'feed' and 'medication' (though not in this country), under conditions which fill one with disquiet. Perhaps it is time that natural materials should be more widespread.

Burntwood
House of Lords
Chairman, National Association
for Health

INTRODUCTION

A miracle food? Can there be such a thing — a panacea for many ills, a safe aid to slimming, wonderful in the kitchen, good for animals — and not expensive.

My own researches into the effects of cider vinegar began in 1956 when I was frankly sceptical of apparently wild and baseless claims. Previously my work had been with the development of pharmaceuticals. I was aware of the controlled experiments and weight of evidence to be produced before claims could be made. Nonetheless, friends and friends of friends kept coming forward with reports of relief from long-standing complaints, with fatness going down on diets somehow suddenly simpler to obey. Complexions improved, the basic functions became once more normal. Perhaps, then that is the key idea behind cider vinegar therapy — to make normal.

Cider vinegar will not work in every way for every person, there are those who it simply upsets, those who find no effect at all — and those who find opening for them a wonderful new chapter in a life which had begun to fail in quality.

Orthodox medicine has in recent years greatly increased our chances of attaining middle age and nowhere would I wish my reader to avoid seeking medical advice when this is needed. But cider vinegar is not a drug, it is not normally antagonistic to other treatments. It is suitable for diabetics, for people on low salt diets, little children, old people and even animals.

Where the orthodox ideas have failed is in substantially increasing the life expectancy of the middle aged. We have only a 5 year improvement for men and 8 years for women aged 45, in the past century. I believe that a main cause of this is poor nutrition. Whilst three-quarters of the world suffers from malnutrition most of the rest suffer in a different way; from over-nutrition. Cider vinegar appears to provide certain minerals and other elements needed by a very large number of almost healthy individuals.

My purpose in writing this book is to pass on to you the long and critical experience I have had in using and recommending cider vinegar. To tell you of the reasons why more than 1,000 regular users find real benefit. I shall let you come with me in your imagination around the main places where it is produced in Britain so that you know exactly what real cider vinegar is and the questions to ask when offered a new make. You will be able to try cider vinegar for culinary use with the wonderful and practical recipes I have collected. You will be guided in your efforts to become slim and I shall even provide a beauty secret or two.

None of this would have been possible without two great pioneers in the use of cider vinegar — Cyril Scott, the eminent composer, mystic and practical healer who first introduced it to Britain in 1948 with a book called *Cider Vinegar* and Dr. D.C. Jarvis who followed up his articles in the American magazine *The Medical World* with his two revealing books on the effectiveness of Vermont country medicine, *Folk Medicine* and *Arthritis and Folk Medicine*. Dr. Jarvis published his first book in 1960. Since then many more case histories have been reported and more uses discovered. Many hundreds of friends and correspondents have asked me to recommend a comprehensive and up-to-date survey of cider vinegar. It is for them that I write this book and also in the hope that countless more will be happier and healthier as a result.

CHAPTER ONE

HOW CIDER VINEGAR IS MADE

In time past, cider vinegar was cider that had 'gone wrong'. Today, such is the need for a reliable and effective product that there is no such easy way out for the producers. The three main brands, Applefords, Martlet and Whiteways, use a basically similar method with certain differences which I shall point out where appropriate. All these firms have been most helpful in the compilation of this chapter and, indeed, in revealing helpful details from their private files regarding special uses and effects.

The apples arrive in September and October. Lorries full of freshly picked, specially grown, apples in the peak of condition. At Applefords the main crop is from the shiny Somerset cider apple, so full of minerals and acidity that it is not really possible to eat, even cooked with raw sugar! Martlet specialize in the firm fruity Bramley from the Kent and Sussex orchards, full of flavour and fragrance. Whiteways use Devon apples, not perhaps so tart as those from Somerset, but producing an excellent cider.

Until recently, after the whole apples had been coarsely chopped, they would be fed into hydraulic presses which sent volumes of delectable fresh apple juice coursing into cool, underground vats. The once-pressed pulp was then transferred to another press and squeezed until the apples became almost dry. Today, the apples go through an enormous rotary and continuous press which extracts the juice even more surely than the presses of old. When the apple remains reach the end, all the juice has gone and what is left is sent to be converted into organic compost or apple pectin. This is the setting agent used to provide the right consistency in good jams and conserves. I have always found it good to know that the apple is so completely used for our health, nutrition and good eating.

The apple juice goes then into large vats, usually of Russian oak because only those huge trees provide perfect staves of sufficient length and quality. A culture of yeast begins the fermentation which completely changes all the sugar in the apple juice into alcohol. The time this takes depends upon the temperature and on certain other factors, but is about 3-4 weeks. After this, cider needs to mature for about six months — much longer than the four or five weeks needed for beer in a brewery — and then we are ready to make the vinegar.

The final process is called acetification. The traditional process, which is now superseded, was to acetify in huge 20,000 gallon vats made of Columbian pine or New Zealand Kauri pine although there was no reason why the stainless steel or fibre glass vats or glass lined steel vats which are replacing them should not be just as good. The vat had a web of lathes upon which sterilized four-feet layers of birch twigs were put until the vat contained some two tons of twigs. These were steamed for forty-eight hours prior to use. The twigs were then soaked in alcohol from cider mixed with some vinegar that was from a freshly working vat. This allowed the micro-organism, a bacterium called *Acetobacter* to become well established on the birch twigs. The cider was then added in 5,000 gallon batches and circulated through the acetifier for two or three weeks. This allowed plenty of oxygen to be present which is necessary for the acetobacter to convert entirely the alcohol into acetic acid. When this process had been completed the vinegar was lightly filtered into storage vats, of aged oak, where it developed flavour and any sediment was thrown.

Today, the invention of the '*Fring's Acetator*' has speeded up the changing of alcohol into acetic acid without any loss of quality. In fact, there is every chance that quality is increased in modern cider vinegars because the enclosed Fring's process very much reduces the loss of the vital ingredients by evaporation, which often occurred in the traditional method.

In the *Fring's Acetator* the *Acetobacter* grows in a suspension of fine air bubbles and fermenting liquid. This causes a very even distribution of the *Acetobacter* through the cider and the change, under carefully controlled conditions, takes only a few days. Half the tank is usually ready to use whilst the other half is being transformed, so the result is a more or less continuous supply of high quality cider vinegar. Both processes produce an acetic acid content which depends on the efficiency of the equipment but is usually around 7 per cent. This is far too strong for normal use so it is then diluted to about 4.8 per cent before being bottled. (See analyses for further information.)

Once in the bottle, it is important that the vinegar does not oxydize or grow moulds. For this reason it is necessary to add a substance which deters the oxygen from affecting the vinegar. The usual substance is sulphur dioxide. This was first known to have been used some 2,000 years ago by the ancient Greeks who burnt sulphur in the top of barrels of wine before sealing them down. The U.K. Food Laws state that the maximum allowable content of sulphur dioxide in cider vinegar is 70 parts per million, which is one of the lowest permitted figures for food products.

Appleford's cider apple vinegar has now, and for some time past, successfully replaced the sulphur dioxide by the incorporation of vitamin C (ascorbic acid) and it is certain the other makers will, as Whiteways has, adopt this positively healthy approach to preservation.

Martlet cider vinegar is sold in its natural colour, which is light straw. Applefords, on the other hand, found that their production methods caused some variations in colour and therefore control the final shade of brown by the addition of a little burnt sugar caramel.

For the technically minded, the change of the alcohol into vinegar (acetic acid) follows this chemical chain:

$$CH_3CH_2OH \xrightarrow{-2H} CH_3CHO \xrightarrow{(0)} CH_3COOH$$

ethyl alcohol   acetaldehyde   acetic acid

The greatest possible yield is 1.3 grams of acetic acid from 1.0 gram of alcohol and this is nearly reached in modern equipment.

The great mystery is why these changes to cider that transform it to cider vinegar also create such a remarkable aid to health for so many people.

CHAPTER TWO

CHOOSING THE RIGHT CIDER VINEGAR

As you will have read in the chapter on how cider vinegar is made, in simple terms cider vinegar is just vinegar made from cider. The shopper has many makes to choose from. Which is the best for him?

In Britain there are three main producers, Appleford's, Martlet and Whiteways, plus one small producer, Chevalier Guild. These are all makers of different cider vinegars of the very highest quality. The main producers all also do some bottling for other firms. Quite soon it will be necessary to make it clear on the label if the contents are imported. The tests and results of this book were all made using British cider vinegars. Dr. Jarvis has obtained good results with his American products. I cannot speak for those made in other lands except to say that analyses of Swiss cider vinegar imported into Britain show a marked reduction in the mineral content. For example, the amount of potassium in the Swiss product is approximately half the British. Therefore beware of vinegars where the shopkeeper cannot tell you if they are British or from abroad. As I said, the only acceptable alternative supply appears to be American, at least until many more tests are carried out.

Cows suffer from mastitis from time to time. This disease is caused by a similar type of bacterium to that which often gives us sore throats. It is called *streptococcus mammitis*. This bacterium can be grown in the laboratory on a nutritive jelly so that the effects of different antiseptics can be tested. It is a most remarkable fact that *streptococcus mammitis* is *killed* with cider vinegar. However, the *streptococcus* is *not* harmed by malt vinegar or by cider itself. Research has not yet discovered why cider vinegar has this special and unique effect among the tested substances. On the other hand, scientific research has not yet established why it is that vitamin C (ascorbic acid) is essential for health. We know only that it *is* essential. The contents of this book are based then on experimental evidence and observations which, when added together, support most strongly the belief that cider vinegar provides a factor which is conducive to improved general health. This does not mean that cider vinegar will help every single one of those who have the conditions, complaints and illnesses dealt with in this book. But the number who find it works for them is so large that the cider vinegar treatment can be looked upon as a natural, effective, inexpensive and, above all, safe remedy. It does not conflict with other treatments. I must emphasize that qualified advice must be sought and acted upon if you believe a condition to be serious or potentially serious. No book can take the place of a consultation — you cannot have medicine by mail order! However, you may well find, as many have, that the suggestions in this volume will positively and easily help you to enjoy a better quality of life. I shall be most interested to learn of any exceptional results especially if they could help others in the future.

Whiteways call their vinegar 'cyder', whilst Martlet and Appleford's call theirs 'cider'. Although Whiteways are probably Britain's oldest producer, they have been making it for more than 100 years, the 'cyder' spelling is not significant. In fact from the earliest times writers have been in two minds (or more) over the spelling. Neither is incorrect, as you will find if you examine the history of the name. There was a late Latin word *sicera*, which meant intoxicating liquor or strong drink. This was often used in the Bible of that time. In due course the word became altered, first to *sizra* and then to *sidra*.

Apples are a native fruit of Britain, in fact it is thought to be one of the only fruits to spread from East to West. There may well have been cultivated orchards in Britain since Neolithic times for cider making. In the thirteenth-century the bailiff's account of the Earl of Devon's estate at Exminster showed a large production of cider. In 1724, Daniel Defoe, of *Robinson Crusoe* fame, wrote that 'Between Topsham and Axminster so much fruit grew and so much cider was made that sometimes they send to London between ten and twenty thousand hogshead of cider each year'. A hogshead is approximately 60 gallons. No doubt cider making began on a large scale as a way of preserving the goodness of apples and, indeed, vitamin C, through the winter months.

Literature began to refer commonly to cider in the fourteenth-century. Interesting references include the following:

1398 – Trevisa wrote, 'Honey cometh of floures, sidre of frute and ale of corne'.

1497 – Bishop Alcock wrote, 'Saynt John Baptyst wich ete neuer flesshe, dranke no wyne nor cydre'.

1626 – Francis Bacon wrote about sider; in 1663 Boyle talked of syder and perry.

1708 – J. Phillips wrote, 'My mill now grinds choice apples and the British vats o'erflow with generous cider'.

1767 – Hutchinson wrote, 'A barrel full of cyder'. In his *History of England* at about the same time, Macaulay recorded, 'Hogsheads of their best cyder'.

1875 – Jevons wrote, 'The farm labourer may partially receive payment in cider'.

So the different spellings change from age to age and run simultaneously together without there being a particular regional or other significance. You can therefore use, with a clear conscience, cyder *or* cider vinegar!

The cost has, considering the general way in which money has been devalued over the last 65 years, remained remarkably modest. In 1906, Whiteways listed apple vinegar in champagne bottles at a trade price of 7/6d (37½ new pence) a dozen. The larger sizes, which are by far the most economical if you use a lot, are perhaps 10-15 times as much today. When you remember that a goodish working wage was £50 a year in 1907, cider vinegar becomes one of today's bargains.

THE BASIC TREATMENT

The standard way in which I recommend the taking of cider vinegar is to mix two teaspoonsful in a tumbler of cold or warm water. Take one glassful first thing in the morning, one during or after lunch and one in the evening.

Different users find that different makes of cider vinegar work best for them so, if the first one you try does not seem to produce the hoped-for results, then try another. Some people with sensitive stomachs may find two teaspoonsful too much for them. In such cases, start with one teaspoonful until you are used to the effects. Children under the age of about eight years also usually find the small dose sufficient. Infants can, of course, use less still but many babies and children really enjoy vinegar! A sweet tooth tends to be developed by the parents because they associate sweetness with reward. This is not to the advantage of a child's health — a 'vinegar tooth' is far better with a preference for savoury foods.

HONEY AND CIDER VINEGAR

Dr. Jarvis recommends for many cases a mixture of honey and cider vinegar. The ideal seems to be equal volumes of the two ingredients. By weight this is equivalent to 42 per cent. of cider vinegar and 58 per cent. of honey. This is very much an individual thing. Many who find cider vinegar either upsetting their stomach or not working well, find the mixture, which can be obtained in a prepared form, the perfect answer. If you mix your own, be sure to use an unblended pure honey. It does not matter if it is set or clear. Do *not* heat the mixture, as this is not good for certain constituents. The mixture is especially effective for hay fever and for asthma. My own view is that the honey helps the absorption, in certain cases, besides being itself valuable.

CHAPTER THREE

THE COMPOSITION OF CIDER VINEGAR

The active principles in cider vinegar come from the combination of minerals, organic matter and acetic acid in a naturally produced blend. There are certain to be fluctuations from time to time because of variations in the apple. In general the cider apple vinegars, Applefords and Whiteways, have a higher potassium content whilst the Bramley apple product has a higher acetic acid content. This is why different vinegars suit different persons depending upon the balance required.

The figures quoted are in grammes (g) per 100 millilitres (ml) or, where appropriate, in milligrammes (mg) or parts per million (p.p.m.).

For the general reader this information is not of much importance but as, so far as I can ascertain, it has not previously been published in book form, the analyses are included to make this survey as comprehensive as possible. Where I do not have specific information, this has been left out. This does not mean that the substance is actually absent.

Applefords — analysis per 100 mls.

Total solid matter	3.31 g
Acetic acid	4.75 g
Sugars (as invert)	0.45 g

Mineral ash	0.32 g
Tannins	0.015 g
Calcium	8.2 mg
Phosphorus	4.85 mg
Sodium	7.0 mg
Potassium	120.0 mg
Ascorbic Acid (vitamin C)	100.0 p.p.m.
Riboflavin (vitamin B2)	trace
Nicotinic Acid	trace
Iron	0.05 p.p.m.
Copper	0.025 p.p.m.

Martlet — analysis per 100 mls.

Total solid matter	1.36 g
Acetic Acid	5.40 g
Sugars (as invert)	0.40 g
Mineral ash	0.24 g
Tannins	0.002 g
Protein	0.08 g
Calcium	7.1 mg
Phosphorus	6.5 mg
Sodium	12.0 mg
Potassium	103.0 mg
Iron	1.3 mg
Lead	nil
Arsenic	nil
Copper	0.54 p.p.m.
Zinc	0.10 p.p.m.
Riboflavin (vitamin B2)	trace
Nicotinic Acid	0.02 mg

Whiteways — analysis per 100 mls.

| Total Solid matter | 3.29 g |

Acetic Acid	4.80 g
Sugars (as invert)	0.48 g
Sugar Free Dry Extract	2.80 g
Mineral Ash	0.30 g
Tannins	0.061 g
Protein	0.05 g
Calcium	8.0 mg
Phosphorus	4.8 mg
Sodium	7.0 mg
Potassium	120.0 mg
Iron	0.5 mg
Lead	nil
Arsenic	nil
Copper	0.2 p.p.m.
Zinc	nil
Riboflavin (vitamin B2)	trace
Nicotinic Acid	trace
Ascorbic Acid (vitamin C)	100 p.p.m.

I mention elsewhere that imported Swiss cider vinegar has a much lower potassium content than the British, about 70 mg per 100 mls, in fact. It is not unlikely that the other minerals are also low.

The analyses of these three main makes of vinegar are entirely satisfactory for our purposes. It all depends which suits you as to which you use.

CHAPTER FOUR

CIDER VINEGAR FOR HEALTH

Describing the remarkable results of cider vinegar in a variety of complaints, one day, a friend said to me, in a scathing tone, 'Cider Vinegar seems to cure everything except corns!' It is true that the use is very wide in application. But, to draw a lesson from my friend's rebuke, I would say to you that corns do not usually trouble people with perfect shoes. In the same way, illness is minimized in a perfectly fit body. Fitness comes from having sufficient exercise, enough sleep, a realistic and positive attitude of mind and *a well managed diet*. I believe that cider vinegar contains minute quantities of minerals which help to adjust our metabolism, or bodily processes, that are frequently missing when we eat.

It is for this reason that cider vinegar has been called a panacea. Not because it has a strong drug-like action with unwelcome and often unsuspected side effects, but because cider vinegar makes the body normal.

Also for this reason cider vinegar cannot be guaranteed to work every time for everybody. But it *does* work, and work marvellously, for hundreds and thousands of men, women and children throughout the world.

Dr. Jarvis carried out some experiments on

cows to see if, as had been thought, it was the phosphorus in cider vinegar which was the vital and required element. It was not, and the final answer must await trials which will cost a great deal of money to carry out and which will not alter the fact which you can profit by straight away — that it really works for a very large number of people.

I mentioned earlier that over a thousand people had helped to establish some real and basic information by telling me why they used cider vinegar successfully. This work was done with Appleford's Cider Apple Vinegar. Martlet have carried out successful controlled trials using a mixture of honey and cider vinegar for the treatment of hay fever and of asthma. Martlet, Whiteways and Applefords have each much experience in the veterinary uses. It is for me this last usage, for animals that convinces me that the use of cider vinegar is not strange or unreasonable. I simply do not believe that animals can be fooled into health through cider vinegar. They recover because it works and, if it works for them, why should it not for us?

I will discuss the results of the survey and the recommended dosages under each category of complaint but, for the sake of interest, here are the various uses and the number of users in each main section:

General Health (Vigour, happiness, etc.) 426
General Qualities and Benefits 214
Slimming 184

Cooking	38
Rheumatism	39
Arthritis	39
'Flu, Colds, Catarrh, Sore Throat	16
Wrinkles	2
Blood Purification	2
Hay Fever	14
Toe and Finger Nails	4
Backache	4
Varicose Veins	4
Asthma	11
Skin Troubles	2
Insomnia	7
Digestive Disturbances	34
Cataract	1
Heart Troubles	17
Cramp	4
Shingles	5
High Blood Pressure	12
	1,079

Remember, as you read the descriptions of the various complaints, that they are *all* based on actual and recent case histories supported by 'the experience of previous writers and users over very many years'. Also, I will take this opportunity of thanking Appleford's, Martlet and Whiteways for the help they have given in the compilation of what is the first comprehensive book on cider vinegar therapy. But we must also thank them for making this remarkable food available. Other countries also have cider vinegars of great quality. Check with the analytical chapter if you are not in Britain and find a type to suit you and your body's needs.

SLIMMING

Life assurance companies have known for a long time from their carefully kept records that fatness and health do not often go together.

Fatness does not look very attractive, at least not to Western eyes, and more children are unable to adjust to a happy school relationship with their fellows because they are ungraceful and ungainly fatties.

Cider vinegar helps you to achieve a normal diet. It improves the functioning and adjustment of the body so that there is efficient use made of the food you eat and you become very satisfied and content with the right amount.

Before embarking on your slimming with cider vinegar be sure to examine your present diet to see that it is well balanced and healthy. Cider vinegar can do a lot for you, but it is better if you provide yourself with the right nutritious diet as well. Check yourself:

1. Do I eat wholemeal bread and flour products? (Remember, doctors and surgeons have recently discovered that diseases of the colon, or lower part of the gut, are made worse through over-refined foods and improve, or are avoided, with wholemeal.)
2. Do I eat too much sugar? (The average intake of sugar in the U.K. is about 120 pounds a year. That is for every man, woman and child. I know I don't have my

share, so many must have far more. Sugar,
apart from making you fat, helps cause
tooth decay, affects the blood and may
cause heart trouble in some people.)

3. Am I sure to eat some green vegetable and
some fruit each day? (Fruit, especially
citrus, provides vitamin C. Vegetables are
best lightly cooked or steamed in the
minimum of water. Use the stock for soups
as it contains water soluble vitamins and
minerals.)

4. Do I include protein in my daily diet?
(Protein builds muscles and repairs the
cells. It cannot be stored for long so is
needed daily. Proteins come from nuts,
soya beans, milk, eggs, cheese, fish and lean
meat.)

5. Do I eat too much salt? (If the circulation
is sluggish, salt tends to increase the reten-
tion of water in the body.)

Right as you are determined to eat for health,
now for slimming the Cider Vinegar way!

FIRST RULE: Start off your day by *sipping*
two teaspoonsful of cider
vinegar in a tumbler of cold
or lukewarm water. Have it
ready by the side of your
bed.

SECOND RULE: Sip a tumbler of water containing the two teaspoonsful
of cider vinegar *during* each
of the three main meals of
the day — breakfast, lunch

and dinner. Try to make your drink last the whole meal through. If you cut out any meal, have the cider vinegar drink instead.

THIRD RULE: Chew your food thoroughly. This is to give the cider vinegar the greatest chance to act.

If you are fat or even a bit overweight, this change in your body did not happen in a week or two. You have grown larger gradually, perhaps over many years. *WARNING! Do not reduce too fast.* If you rush it, not only will your skin sag but you will become overtired and fractious.

Achieving the right weight is a wonderful thing to do. Be happy whilst you slim. This really is possible when you slim with cider vinegar.

Now for some experiences of those who have succeeded and now make cider vinegar a part of their daily routine:

Mrs. E.D., an old age pensioner from Shrewsbury writes:

'I have taken 2 tsp. of cider vinegar with each meal for 8-9 months, not bothering when out or looking after guests. Last month I lost another 2 lb. making 17 lb. over the period.'

Mrs. M.D., of Perthshire, Scotland, says:

'I have been taking cider vinegar daily for six months and have lost 21 pounds.'

It was Miss J.B., of Ripon, who said:

'Cider vinegar is a girth's best friend!', which is an amusing truth which applies not only to girls but also to men. For example, Mr. C.F-G., of Glamorgan, found he not only lost weight but improved in general health. A male nurse, Mr. C.F., of Bournemouth, found the answer to be cider vinegar, after a long battle with obesity. Mr. J.S. of Belfast, was embarrassed by his 'pot' when he went swimming but now he looks fine once again.

As long as you keep the **THREE RULES** you can confidently expect to slim, even if you fail to reform your diet, but how much better to do both.

Miss S.B., of London, S.E.3, found that she could slim *without* that most difficult attribute — will power! Mr. A.H.E., of Frinton-on-Sea, said that cider vinegar worked wonders for him without any exercise at all, although my own view is that slimming comes with cider vinegar but a good shape from a mixture of heredity and exercise. If you were born with a tendency to podgy thighs there is always the possibility that when you slim enough to have gorgeous thighs, you will have a skinny neck or hollow cheeks. I am sure that slow slimming, the cider vinegar way, minimizes these problems, whereas rapid slimming aggravates them.

As extra bonus was pointed out to me by Mrs. M.P., of Chesterfield, when she remarked that she had tried dozens of slimming methods without success but when she used the cider

vinegar way it not only worked, it was economical. She was supported by very many others,
including Mrs.G.F., of Kings Norton, who said
that cider vinegar lost weight for her without
any diet at all.

In this connection I would say that she is not
quite right. You see, we are all on a diet, you,
me, our friends. The problem is whether or not
it is the right diet for you. It is not wise to
generalize because human needs are a very
personal thing but one thing is certain, in
many, many peoples' diet, cider vinegar is very
effective indeed for the normalization of
weight. So, if that is your problem, start right
away. As I go about meeting people, I shall be
very interested to hear how you progress.

ARTHRITIS AND RHEUMATISM

Arthritis

My interest in the cider vinegar therapy for
arthritis was awakened many years ago when I
found that one of my thumbs had suddenly
become so weak that I could not lift a jug or a
dinner plate. The Royal National Orthopaedic
Hospital took X-rays and removed much blood
for blood tests. I had osteo-arthritis. I mixed
myself a 'natural cocktail' — a tumbler of warm
water in which I dissolved two teaspoons each
of cider vinegar and molasses and one of pure
unblended honey. Within three months I was
better and have not had a recurrence since, and
that is about twelve years ago. Spontaneous

remissions are always possible. But in my mind a spontaneous remission is a result of the body winning a fight against disease, not just luck.

In the intervening years I have found people who do not get on with the mixture I used. They find cider vinegar alone or cider vinegar and honey the best for them. Others just use crude black molasses with good results, yet others fail to obtain relief, but in my experience among arthritics they are a minority.

The first point to remember is that if there has been a great change in the bone through calcium deposits caused by arthritis, then it is not at all likely that this will be altered. The second thing to remember is that 'a cure' is probably too much to hope for or to expect. Look for control of symptoms, easing of pain and a reduction in the development of the condition. Keep as mobile as possible and above all do not give up hope. The longer you have had arthritis, the longer it is likely to be before you obtain a helpful result. Charles Walker, an old friend of mine, relates how when he owned a Health Store in Birkenhead, an elderly man came in one day and danced round the shop. When questioned, he said he was not going crazy, he was demonstrating that he *could* dance. Two years before he had visited the store in a wheel-chair, crippled with arthritis. He had taken cider vinegar and molasses for two years and felt ten years younger! Not everyone can expect such results, but they are at least a matter of common experience.

Dr. Jarvis recommends for arthritis:

1. Two teaspoonsful cider vinegar and two of honey in a glass of water, taken at each meal, or if not acceptable, between meals.
2. On Monday, Wednesday and Friday add one drop of iodine at one meal to the mixture.
3. One kelp tablet at breakfast or at all three meals.
4. Avoidance of wheat foods and cereals, white sugar, citrus fruits, muscle meats such as beef, lamb and pork, as these produce an adverse reaction.

He says this regime helps rheumatoid arthritis, osteo-arthritis, bursitis and gout.

I have no quarrel with these procedures but wonder if the dietary restrictions in fact make much difference. As you will have read, I believe that the addition of molasses helps because of the great cleansing power of that food, so my recommendation for arthritis is:

1. On rising, two teaspoonsful of cider vinegar in a tumbler of water.
2. With each meal, two teaspoons each of cider vinegar and molasses with one of honey, sipped during the meal in a tumbler of water.
3. A natural vitamin and mineral supplement each day.
4. A diet very low in sugar and refined flour.

Mrs. D.T. of Pinner, who has a spine that has had to be surgically fixed together, is now free from pain by following this treatment. After years of pain she finds the feeling of relief unbelievable.

Mr. F.N. of Willenhall writes: 'Not only has cider vinegar, honey and molasses helped my arthritis but for general health it is so good that people ask me where I get my energy from (I am 80 years old).'

Mr. J.J. of Edinburgh says that he no longer requires the use of drugs or a collar since taking cider vinegar alone.

Mrs. F.S. of London, S.E.11, found that although she is almost crippled with arthritis, cider vinegar was a great help in keeping it under control.

Mrs. M.S. of Rotherham found that mixing cider vinegar with honey brought her quick relief, whereas Mrs. M.H. of Tuffley, found that cider vinegar with molasses gave her the most effective relief from pain.

When a doctor uses modern drugs in the treatment of arthritis he is involved with many problems such as controlling the side-effects of cortisone or the gastric problems of aspirin. You have none of these difficulties when employing the cider vinegar method, although it must be stated that in intractable cases the whole armoury of medicine in skilled hands is needed to make life tolerable for those who suffer from arthritis. Do try to start treatment early on. In this way you may much delay or permanently avoid the development of more serious symptoms and control your condition through safe and natural means.

MUSCULAR RHEUMATISM

This is a muscular condition which may be caused by the build-up of poisons in the muscles or by the failure of the body to remove toxic wastes quickly enough. In general I have found that treatment as for arthritis is usually helpful. I must point out though that they are not the same, as arthritis affects joints and rheumatism the muscles. It tends to be aggravated by draughts and damp clothes.

Ordinary muscular rheumatism is not all that serious, especially if you look after yourself, avoiding excessive exertions to which you are not accustomed.

Mrs. A.P. of Cardiff tells me that with cider vinegar alone she has had great relief from her muscular rheumatism.

Mrs. K.M.C., who found great benefit for her condition, said she was told of it by a very old lady who had known the remedy for 80 years!

Mr. J.M.N. of Barnstaple, was suffering frequently and now takes a dessertspoon each of honey and cider vinegar in water so that it has become a way of life — without any more aches and pains. He goes on to say that his favourite cider vinegar is so mellow, mature and smooth tasting that it can be taken like wine without offending the stomach.

GOUT

Although gout is often associated with rheumatism in peoples' minds, it is likely that it is somewhat different in cause. Modern medicines relieve the acutely painful attack in a way no natural remedy can. The cider vinegar, honey and molasses mixture is, in cases of gout, best taken half as strong and twice as often so that you have a pint of the weaker liquid at each meal. Avoid port and red wine. (Pitt, the statesman, had gout at twenty-one but it is usually a problem of middle age.) Eat little muscle meat, no sardines or roe. Plenty of whole grain foods and fresh fruit. If you really have to drink alcohol, whisky and water appears to be statistically preferable for there is a very low incidence of gout in Scotland.

NOSE AND THROAT DISORDERS

Colds
Not only does the common cold and its complications cause a great deal of time to be taken from work, it also usually makes the sufferer a misery to himself and a threat to others.

Professor Linus Pauling of the U.S.A. has written of the good effects of very large doses of vitamin C in the prevention and treatment of colds. This theory has been supported by recent trials in British and Canadian universities. Although the long term physical effects of these large doses are not yet finally established, Professor Pauling believes that we all need more vitamin C than is customary and suggests we keep it on the table in powder form to sprinkle over our food and put into drinks. I find 1,000 milligrams (1 gram) of vitamin C a day very helpful but when exposed to colds or at the beginning of one, I increase the dose to 1 gram every three hours. This can, with great advantage, be taken in the cider vinegar drink.

The vitamin C therapy does not work with everyone. An American put on a play in London not long ago and the producer wished to avoid, as it was a winter opening, the problem of having colds among the cast. An actor who appeared in the show told me that in spite of injections of vitamin C, plus large daily doses of tablets, this was the only play he has ever appeared in which had to close down for several nights because of the epidemic of colds among cast and understudies alike! But it does work for most people, especially with cider vinegar, at least to minimize the symptoms. For others cider vinegar alone reduces the number of colds, probably by building up the general bodily strength.

Coughs

If you have a mild cough it is a good idea to have a glass of double strength cider vinegar drink, that is, four teaspoonsful of cider vinegar to a glass of water. Swallow a few small sips slowly when the cough is aggravating. This often brings relief and at night permits sleep. Mr. T.B. of Hailsham, has rid himself of night cough after many months by means of this treatment.

Laryngitis

Cyril Scott recommends as a miraculous treatment, one teaspoonful of the cider vinegar to half a glass of water every hour for seven hours. It is also a valuable precautionary measure when you are exposed to infection. I find a little honey added to the mixture most helpful.

Sore Throat

The bacteria often responsible for sore throats prefer an alkaline environment and this may be the reason why the same treatment as for laryngitis works well. If my throat is sore or relaxed after too much talking and especially if I have to address a group of people or, as happened once, I was scheduled to make a television recording about health foods when my voice was not much more than a whisper, I find it is essential to have a first-aid way of avoiding embarrassment even if only for a short time. This first-aid is a special gargle which gives instant relief that is usually maintained for up to three-quarters of an hour. To make it, take:

Special Gargle for the Throat

    10 ounces cider vinegar
     4 ounces honey
     1 ounce red sage (garden sage, *Salvia officinalis*)
     ½ ounce self-heal (*Prunella vulgaris*)
Heat the cider vinegar with the herbs until it is

almost, but not quite, boiling. (Make sure that the pan is *not* aluminium.) Allow to cool slowly. Strain after twenty-four hours, add the honey, stir until dissolved, bottle and cap securely. Use two teaspoonsful in half a glass of water.

Catarrh
Many users have found cider vinegar to assist the clearance of catarrh. Take the basic drink of two teaspoons in a glass of water three times daily but, in addition, put a couple of inches of pure cider vinegar in a small stainless steel or enamel saucepan, simmer it gently and inhale the vapours for five or ten minutes. This procedure brings relief which often lasts up to eight hours.

Nose Bleeding
Because cider vinegar is an astringent it is worth trying in the same way as for catarrh in cases of persistent nose bleeding.

NERVES, CHOKING NERVOUS COUGH
The helpful effects of cider vinegar in many cases of insomnia due to tension are well recognized but an extension of this use as a relaxing beverage came to my notice recently and I cannot do better than quote from the letter written by Miss L.E.B. of Edinburgh:

'I would like to give you an unsolicited testimonial for cider vinegar, for it has literally given me a new lease of life.

Although I had been on a course of molasses for six years, I thought I would start taking cider apple vinegar with my main meal.

For 30 years I have never had a single meal without CHOKING and going blue in the face. My throat would just close right up. Sometimes I could manage half-way through a meal, but it always ended up the same. Consequently, I lost friends, people stopped asking me out and I was a nuisance to myself and everyone else. During the war in the services I had to stand by and see someone else eating my rations because I could not swallow.

One night about a year and a half ago, I was sitting alone and eating my evening meal when it suddenly came to me *I was not choking any more*! I can never tell you what this meant to me — catch *me* going on a diet! I have eaten everything that has been put in front of me since if I take two teaspoonful in water with my meal. In fact I like my food better if I take the vinegar with it — I can go anywhere, cafes, other peoples' homes. I have joined a Burn's Club and we have gone all over the place during the past 12 months and I have had no trouble at all. Perhaps, if you know of other sufferers like myself, recommend cider vinegar. The doctor said it was nerves but thanks to cider vinegar all is now well and I am making up for lost time.'

This very interesting report does demon-

strate the profound balancing and normalizing
effect of cider vinegar in a most human
situation. When you are afflicted by nerves and
tensions try not to resort to habit-forming and
mentally exhausting drugs such as phenobarbi-
tone. They are the cause of increasing national
and international concern for, while they are a
blessing to some who are suffering extreme
pressures or tensions, they are too freely given
in cases where a natural remedy, such as cider
vinegar, will give relief without risk of any sort.

INSOMNIA AND ASTHMA

This section is about ordinary sleeplessness not
resulting from pain or illness. Drugs do not
usually *cure* insomnia. They just desensitize the
mind for a while, often leaving a 'hang-over'
next morning. I have written of the dangers of
the indiscriminate use of powerful habit-
forming drugs. Even less strong medicines can
have their dangers. Think of the thalidomide
children, for example.

Good sleep is nature's great restorative.
Some people, as did Napoleon, are able to
make do with three or four hours each night.
For most of us, though, it occupies about
one-third of our entire lives, so we had best
learn to do it well.

The effects of sleep are felt on the majority
of our bodily functions. The first sign is a
deepening of the breathing and a slowing of the
heart beat. The blood pressure falls. The body
temperature drops by about half a Fahrenheit

degree (or a quarter Centigrade). Your feet grow warmer and your hands colder. The sweat glands are very busy, so good ventilation is necessary. The blood supply to the brain does not decrease. Indeed, your brain is active at night. About an hour after you fall asleep, the pupils of your eyes move quite rapidly. This movement appears to be an essential component of really refreshing sleep and its onset and duration is delayed if sedative drugs are used.

What then can we learn from all this to help our slumbers? Firstly as night approaches, you must cultivate quite consciously a peaceful frame of mind. Think of good things and nice people. Some gentle music often helps. It will be good if you have taken a little exercise in the open air — a short walk, perhaps, brisk enough to tire you a little. Remember that people need differing amounts of sleep although this is inconvenient if your marriage partner needs twice (or half) as much as you do!

In any case, as you grow older you tend to need *less* sleep.

Next it is good to have a warm nourishing drink half-an-hour before retiring. Just before going to bed sip half a tumbler of cider vinegar and honey, 2 teaspoons of each, in warm water. Lie down, think pleasant thoughts, relax your body starting at the toes and going right through the frame until the fingertips are relaxed — breathe deeply and regularly. Do not be worried about *not* sleeping – do not be worried about anything at all – there is nothing you can do to change things in the middle of the night anyway.

Make sure your bedroom is warm enough. Breathing very cold or damp air is bad for the chest and aggravates bronchitis, especially amongst senior citizens. They have, too, a peculiar problem. As the kidneys age, the water they pass to the bladder becomes less and less strong, so there is more of it! Drinking less is quite the worst thing to do. Your kidneys *need* the water to carry on the process of excretion. Just resign yourself to maybe having to rise a couple of times in the night. Take a few more sips of the honey/cider vinegar combination and go peacefully back to sleep again. Many older people read a book in the night or do a few little chores. Just make sure, when you leave your bed, that you do not become chilled.

If you cannot sleep because of pain, grief or illness, then you may need the care and advice of a qualified practitioner who is in a position to advise upon your individual needs.

ASTHMA

In times passed this used to be called the Devil's Disease. Happily, the majority of sufferers are now able to obtain relief from the worst symptoms and often, when the cause is an allergy, a complete cure. Yet others have a spontaneous cessation, or it may be supplanted by hay fever. On the other hand, asthma, although it is most common amongst children and young adults, sometimes does not appear until the forties.

During an attack the person has a feeling of tightness in the throat and neck with perhaps a frightening feeling of suffocation. Breathing is difficult, especially breathing out. Sticky mucus, which later becomes thin, is coughed up when the attack usually ends with a feeling of extreme tiredness.

It is caused by a sudden reduction in diameter of the small tubes in the lungs combined with the production of a lot of mucus. The patient wheezes because of the difficulty of forcing air out through these narrow tubes.

Why the tubes become narrow is a more difficult question. There are three recognized reasons: firstly, an attack of bronchitis sometimes starts asthma off; secondly, asthma can be an allergic reaction to a particular pollen or type of dust, for example; thirdly, it can be inherited from forbears with asthma or hay fever or nettle rash.

The cider vinegar treatment with honey (2 teaspoons of each in a tumbler of water thrice daily) has produced some remarkable results which are presently the subject of long-term experiments. It is certainly worth trying but also it is important for the sufferer to avoid aggravating his own condition by adopting a life as free as possible from stresses and strains and by not placing himself in the way of any causative factors which experience has previously indicated. Smoking is best abandoned. Fatness, or even slight overweight, throws an excessive strain onto the body during an attack, so slim! Happily, an asthmatic lady usually avoids attacks when expecting a child.

Mr. M. McK. of Suffolk 'cured' his longstanding asthma by cider vinegar in water *without* honey, but as most of the experiments have been done with honey, that should be the first preference.

HAY FEVER

The sufferer has what appears to be a very bad summer cold, but there is no infection. Hay fever is caused by sensitization to proteins. We all tend to reject protein of a sort different to our own, that is why tissue transplants are so difficult to carry out effectively. The air is full of pollen protein on a hot summer's day to which many people are acutely sensitive. They pray for rain to keep the pollen count to a bearable level.

Special nasal sprays are sometimes used but these often cause permanent damage to the delicate lining of the nose.

Hay fever is rare in very small infants and tends to reduce in intensity as middle age approaches although it does not often go entirely.

An exception, which is an example well worth following, is Mrs. L.E.G. of Thorpe Bay, who obtained a complete cure by taking, once a day throughout the season, 2 teaspoons each of honey and cider vinegar in a glass of water and, at the same time, cutting out all sugar. When she wrote to me she had been fine for eleven years, having been a very bad sufferer for the previous thirty-four years. Her experience was published in the *Sunday Express*. She subsequently received no less than 4,000 letters and replied to each one! This at least must recommend the therapy! Many of those who tried the method were as successful as she, others were not, but in any case general health and resistance will have been improved.

BEAUTY

The skin, like the eyes, is one of the most obvious places to look for signs of tiredness, age, worry or poor general health. Healthy skin has a bloom and elasticity which, with care, lasts into old age. I do not believe that cider vinegar will bring about a miraculous transformation but those who take it in the usual way for other purposes frequently report a great general improvement in skin tone and appearance which causes them to continue with regular doses.

The reason may lie in the inner cleanliness which is a feature of the treatment. Yellowing eyes are a sign of 'liverishness' and in mild cases cider vinegar taken internally is a great help.

Hair is dead except at the point of growth in the hair follicle but to remain in the best condition it is important to give the scalp a favourable environment. It happens that shampoo is usually alkaline. The scalp, on the other hand, is acid and protected by natural fats. Nature's protection is washed away allowing skin to become scaly and the scalp dry. The balance can be restored by using a cider vinegar rinse after you have shampooed your hair. Many hair stylists use this rinse in preference to the well-known beer rinse because they prefer the cosmetic result. When you add to this the benefit of the treatment to the condition of the scalp you have discovered a reason why so many use cider vinegar externally as well as internally.

There are several ways of using cider vinegar as a beauty treatment, but as few users would wish to smell with an odour more reminiscent of a fish and chip shop than a beauty parlour it is a good plan to make a pleasant infusion. My favourite is:

ROSEMARY CIDER VINEGAR SKIN LOTION

Place 1 ounce of fresh rosemary or ½ ounce dried rosemary in a saucepan with half a pint of water (rain water is best). Bring slowly to the boil, simmer gently for ten minutes, strain, mix with half a pint of cider vinegar. When cool, pour in bottles that can be securely sealed. Store in a dark, cool place.

This makes a fine general purpose lotion. If you wish, by all means add a few drops of eau de-Cologne or perfume. Also other herbs can be used or rose petals even, but rosemary is good for the hair.

You can use the lotion in the following ways:

For a Hair Conditioner — A little poured into the palms of the hands, rubbed vigorously into the scalp with the finger tips.

For a Hair Rinse — A tablespoonful in the final rinsing water makes a wonderful cosmetic rinse.

For the Skin — Dab the lotion on the face very gently, working out from the wrinkles and sagging places.

For Swellings — Some remarkable results are achieved with this lotion or, in fact, just plain cider vinegar, in cases of swellings caused by fatigue, long standing or strained muscles. Apply liberally every hour until the swelling reduces. If you can, make a cold compress from the lotion. This has a very good effect on severe strains. Many peoples' feet and legs swell whilst travelling. The cider vinegar treatment, both internally and externally, is a valuable aid.

VARICOSE VEINS

These must be cared for by a properly qualified person but they are, nevertheless, often most uncomfortable. As Mrs. V.M. of Huddersfield wrote, 'Cider Vinegar gives me great relief for varicose veins'. The treatment cannot be considered in any way a cure but has a beneficial effect nonetheless.

FINGER-NAILS

A doctor can often tell much from an examination of the nails. The white spots which sometimes appear are generally due to a deficiency of calcium. It is a frequent observation that these spots disappear when cider vinegar is being used. This is not because it is a provider of calcium in large amounts, although an appreciable proportion is present, but more especially because it helps the body to make more effective use of the calcium in the diet. Growing children need more calcium than adults and usually obtain it from milk. Older people, on the other hand, find efficient use of sufficient calcium a help in preserving strong bones and in mending them following a fracture.

The nails, then, can show the effects of the cider vinegar treatment in the elimination of white spots. At the same time, some users have reported a general strengthening of thin and brittle nails. Mrs. M.M. of Kingsbury, who was a sufferer from generally weak nails, found relief for the first time after many unsuccessful experiments and her nails are now completely restored. This cannot take place overnight — even a year may be needed before results are apparent, especially with older sufferers from weak nails.

EYES

I have mentioned the better appearance of the eyes frequently noticed as an effect of the treatment. So often we find the physical outward attributes of a user improve as a direct result of the internal benefit of cider vinegar.

Mr. E.A.K. of Portsmouth, reports that he found that a cataract which was forming in one of his eyes stopped progressing by any means so rapidly as before when he took cider vinegar regularly. On the other hand, it must be confessed that this is not a common finding, although not unique, and it may have been a spontaneous slowing-down.

SHINGLES
This is caused by the same virus as chicken pox as parents who have never had chicken pox sometimes find to their anguish when infected by their children. It causes burning pain usually along the path of a nerve. The pain is generally gone with the rash after about a week but occasionally persists. Sufferers, such as Mr. W.C.F. of Lancing, have found neat cider vinegar dabbed regularly upon the sore areas to give far more relief than any medicament. The pain abates quite soon after each treatment but returns after an hour or so, when the application needs to be repeated.

THE DIGESTION
Many digestive disorders arise from a relatively small number of defects. Sometimes the bacteria which work to break down our food for us are of the wrong kind. The problem of too much acidity is not as common as the sellers of

patent alkaline medicines may have you believe. In fact, the *reverse* is often true — sufferers from indigestion may not have enough acid.

When you eat food it goes through a first process of digestion in the mouth where the starches are turned, during the chewing process, into sugar by the enzymes in the saliva. Because chewing helps to break down the food and stimulate the flow of saliva it is important to chew thoroughly. Many of those who live on grain diets, and Eastern philosophers, say chewing each mouthful forty times produces the best results. For my part, I am rather bored a long time before that!

The human saliva is usually alkaline but the active enzyme works best in a slightly acid medium, so we have found our first indication of the value of the cider vinegar drink in that it assists the maintenance of the desired acidity.

After the food has been formed into a conveniently sized portion you swallow it and it descends the eight or nine inches to the stomach which is a collecting sack for the food you eat. The digestive process now carries on a further stage in the stomach. The gastic juices contain about 0.4 per cent. of free hydrochloric acid together with enzymes which make the food liquid. Harmful bacteria and other organisms are usually made harmless whilst the food is in the stomach.

Digestion and absorption of the nutriments continues in the twenty-two feet long small intestine where there are more enzymes and a lot of valuable and essential bacteria which help to break down food into substances which can be absorbed by the body.

These bacteria appear to find, as animal results have shown, much benefit from cider vinegar. One theory, as I mention elsewhere, is that because cider vinegar contains both a high potassium content and acetic acid in apparently balanced amounts, the body is able to convert these raw materials in an entirely natural way into a substance which checks the growth of unwelcome bacteria, allowing the useful types to become more vigorous.

Water is absorbed into the body in the four feet of large intestine where waste matter is accumulated, prior to elimination.

New research by distinguished doctors, including a Fellow of the Royal Society, Dr. Burkitt, and his colleague the surgeon, Mr. Painter, has shown beyond reasonable doubt that for a really healthy digestive system it is necessary to have a quantity of cereal or vegetable fibre daily. The simplest way of taking this is to consume two level tablespoons of bran each day. This can be mixed with a little of the cider vinegar drink or added to your food. The results are remarkable provided the bran treatment is carried on indefinitely.

Having taken care of the general condition of your digestive organs, the specific effects of cider vinegar are themselves of the greatest interest and value.

INDIGESTION

As Mrs. D.A. of Folkestone says, 'Until I took a glassful of the cider vinegar drink with each meal I did not know what it was to experience a meal free from pain and subsequent discomfort.'

Mrs. A.W. of Monmouth suffered from flatulence especially when eating pastry. She found complete relief by adding one teaspoonful of the vinegar to her pastry mix.

Mr. R.E. actually suffered from indigestion due to acidity yet found a daily cider vinegar drink, in spite of being itself acid, an effective answer.

After excessive or unwise eating or drinking the high potassium content is probably a factor in the settling effect obtained by taking the cider vinegar drink. Miss K.S. went on further when she said that she found cider vinegar allowed indulgence without indigestion!

CONSTIPATION

One cricketing enthusiast, Mr. J.A. of Swindon, claims that he is clean bowelled at last, thanks to cider vinegar! This distressing condition cannot be good for you because of the pressures created in the intestine when 'forcing' is necessary I have said that bran is an essential part of this treatment, but cider vinegar is also a great help.

Laxatives are not very good for you, besides being expensive, so try a glassful of water containing 2 teaspoonsful of cider vinegar on rising, during the main meal of the day and before retiring. If this, plus two tablespoonsful of bran each day does not solve your problem by the end of a month, then I would advise your seeking qualified help and advice.

DIARRHOEA

If diarrhoea alternates with constipation you must seek medical assistance, for it is just possible that this is an early warning that all is not well with your gut.

Strawberries affect some people, so do travelling, emotional disturbance and certain conditions or illnesses. The cure is to rectify the cause where this is possible. On the other hand, most diarrhoea is an unfortunate and temporary inconvenience for which cider vinegar is a good first-aid treatment. As one result of diarrhoea is the elimination of much of the water that is usually absorbed by the large intestine, you need plenty of fluids, two or three *extra* pints a day. Add *one* teaspoon of the vinegar to each half pint. Sometimes a kaolin mixture, B.P.C., helps, but the concensus of opinion in simple cases not associated with illness is against most of the travellers' preventive tablets containing clioquinol sold by chemists because of the occasional side-effects.

If an infection is the cause of the problem then you must have the infection treated. The cider vinegar drink can safely be taken in addition to any treatment that is prescribed.

HICCOUGHS

This occurs when your diaphragm is not synchronized properly with the flap which prevents you swallowing air into the stomach. It can arise from a variety of causes. There is a hot, spiced Persian dish called a patia which often starts me off! Normally it goes away within the hour, unless it is due to some more serious condition when the underlying cause should be located and treated. Hiccoughs can be tiring, so it is usual to seek aid if it persists for more than four hours. The cider vinegar first-aid treatment is to sip, very slowly a teaspoonful of undiluted cider vinegar. This usually brings about an immediate cure. If not, try breathing in and out of a paper bag for a minute of two. This creates carbon dioxide which stimulates the breathing centre.

HEARTBURN

A burning sensation behind the breastbone an hour or so after meals is often found to diminish or vanish when cider vinegar is taken with the meal.

HEART CONDITIONS

Heart disease is the main killer of people in the prime of life. Men are vulnerable after the age of thirty-five. Women are usually not likely to have an attack until after the 'change', although the rate is rising.

There is no single cause of this curse of Western civilization, which is only rarely encountered amongst those who live on a natural unprocessed diet, but prevention is easier than cure. Perhaps we know half the causes, so to keep to the rules substantially reduces your risk.

Rules to avoid Heart Attacks

1. If you are not slim, become slim (see chapter on slimming).
2. Avoid sugar and foods made with sugar.
3. Avoid hard fats such as animal fat, coconut and palm oils. Replace them with unsaturated soft fats, such as sunflower seed oil, safflower, soya, corn, olive and fish oils.
4. Take enough exercise to become gently breathless each day; walk upstairs instead of using the lift.
5. Give up smoking.
6. Avoid constipation by taking bran and cider vinegar (see pp. 55). Sometimes older people increase blood pressure temporarily through straining, with bad results.
7. Keep work, recreation, rest and holidays in a sensible balance, after all if you literally work yourself to death you will not be of much use to your family or community.
8. Eat a balanced, mixed diet, taking care not to overcook vegetables or to use too much water.
9. Avoid excessive salt (sodium chloride), the element sodium *in excess* increases the tendency of some people to high blood

pressure.

10. Try to have several small meals each day, not one huge feast which could throw a strain onto the body by increasing greatly the amount of fat in the blood stream.

From the foregoing it is plain that cider vinegar cannot be claimed to prevent, or for that matter to cure, heart troubles or allied disorders. Nevertheless, it can play a part in helping you to achieve or maintain the right weight. Additionally, some individuals find it does give them relief from certain symptoms.

ANGINA

Angina is a condition is which the arteries of the heart do not always pass enough blood. This gives rise to a sometimes suffocating pain in the upper chest which often also affects the left arm and the neck. This is similar to the type of pain often occurring in a coronary heart attack but, with rest, it passes off. Doctors give nitroglycerin tablets which must be chewed and give almost immediate relief. Patients who look after themselves have a good outlook and future.

Mr. R.R. of Kemsing found the cider vinegar drink taken regularly lessened the severity of the attack. But I agree with Mr. E.J. of Blackpool, who, as a sufferer, takes the cider vinegar treatment in order to keep his weight down and so improve his anginal condition.

HIGH BLOOD PRESSURE

This is also called hypertension. Sufferers benefit considerably by adopting the ten rules for avoiding heart attacks.

In their own cases, Mrs. C.W. of Huddersfield and Mrs. F.W. of Newtown found that the cider vinegar drink three times daily helped keep blood pressure down. This is likely to be because of an improvement in their general condition through the treatment.

CRAMP

Cramp is quite common amongst the middle-aged and elderly. It may arise because the muscles suffer from a building up of poisonous wastes which the circulation does not take away with enough speed. A number of sufferers have told me that the cider drink, preferably with honey in warm water, taken before retiring, reduces the frequency of attacks.

BURNS

Use pure, undiluted cider vinegar straight from the bottle to relieve the pain and soreness of minor burns.

Modern treatment for burns advocates very rapid cooling with lots of cold water as soon as a burn occurs. This is even more important when clothes are either burnt or wetted with a hot liquid. Pour cold water over the clothes at once. If it is a bad burn, always summon medical aid. Keep the patient warm and rested with something to drink. Do not remove clothing from, or otherwise disturb, the burnt area. Minor burns benefit from the cider vinegar treatment. When possible, it is best to leave them exposed to the air, provided that the skin is intact.

SUNBURN

The same general rules apply here as for ordinary burns. The cider vinegar dabbed on is most soothing. Really serious cases require medical help. Although cider vinegar is very good for treating sunburn, it is in no sense a preventive. A properly prepared filtering oil or lotion and a good deal of caution are both needed for a really happy holiday in the sun.

TEETH AND MOUTH

I must confess to having little personal experience of cider vinegar for the teeth but Cyril Scott, who still had a good few teeth in his nineties, recommends the use of cider vinegar, one teaspoon in water night and morning, as a mouth wash. He says that the teeth should be brushed with the solution and that cider vinegar drinkers had usually white teeth.

Scott mentions that two tablespoonsful of the vinegar to a kettle of water which is allowed to stand for a time allows the lime deposits to come away when the water is poured off, or it can be more easily scraped away without damaging the inner surface of the kettle.

He uses this as an analogy for dental use and

I would be interested to hear from successful users for this purpose.

Mouth ulcers and sores also benefit from the mouth wash; and for a tendency towards bleeding gums the mouth wash is helpful in addition to the cider vinegar treatment three times a day.

CHAPTER FIVE

CIDER VINEGAR IN THE KITCHEN

If, like me, you are convinced of the health advantages of cider vinegar, then the logical next step is to use it as much as possible. The kitchen offers many wonderful opportunities to use cider vinegar in ways which are a compliment to your good taste.

The chef of one of the most distinguished hotels in London renowned for its cuisine, uses cider vinegar for its flavour in preference to wine or malt vinegar.

My family is not vegetarian, although we much respect the ethical ideals of our vegetarian friends. We are, on the other hand, believers in eating whole foods free so far as possible from any chemical additive. This happily permits gourmet cooking, which is a hobby of mine. My young son Carl, often comes shopping with me. He will not let us buy anything to eat until he has read the list of ingredients to check that there are no synthetics. I commend that practice to you all, especially if you are able to avoid the occasional embarrassment I suffer when another shopper buys some instant wonder, whereupon his powerful and pentrating voice points out to me and to all men the error of her ways!

This cooking section sets out to let you into

some of the delightful and varied uses we have for cider vinegar in our home. It includes some excellent additional recipes from other well-tried sources which are acknowledged in their due place.

Please remember that cider vinegar does sometimes form 'mother of vinegar' if the cap is not replaced tightly. If you are buying a gallon for economic reasons, it is not necessarily going to keep without some possibility of deterioration for a year or more, as some users expect. Six months is a fair life for a large bottle. Even then it is best to decant the gallon size into very clean half or one pint strongly stoppered bottles if you wish to use it over a longish period.

BASIC VINEGARS
Herbal or spiced vinegars are delightful to 'spike' the flavour of savoury dishes. You can also store herbs for the winter in a far more aromatic state than by drying them (although dry herbs have very many uses) by putting them tightly packed into a jar of cider vinegar. When you need the herb, just shake it dry and use in the way you prefer.

For the flavoured vinegars I find it best to buy sufficient small-sized bottles of cider vinegar to provide one for each variety. Be sure to stick an appropriate label on after you have prepared the vinegar. It would be rather a shock to use chilli vinegar as a mouth wash!

BASIC METHOD

The basic methods are similar, except when specified. You remove a little vinegar if necessary, add the appropriate flavouring, re-seal and leave for a few days or a week before using. There is not normally any need to remove the herbs before use, in fact the flavour improves with age. The quantities are right for a 10-13-ounce bottle.

Celery Vinegar — Chop a quarter pound of cleaned root and white stalk, leave for a month. Or use ¼-ounce celery seed instead. A pinch of seed is sometimes preferred in the first recipe. Good with salads.

Chilli Vinegar — Use one or two whole hot red or green chillies. One of each is nice. Dried chillies will do, but are not so full of flavour. Wonderful with fish dishes, curries and oysters.

Cucumber Vinegar — Chop 3 ounces of cucumber, including the skin, together with a shallot or small onion with a crushed peppercorn. Very fragrant and refreshing with salads and cold meat.

Fennel Vinegar — Slice two outside leaves of fennel. You can also add some parsley if you like. Good with mutton and fish.

Fines Herbes Vinegar — This is a famous French general purpose flavoured vinegar. Excellent as a basis for a salad dressing. Use one half-teaspoonful each of whole peppercorns, tarragon and basil, the grated skin of a small lemon, a pinch each of savory, thyme, sea salt and raw sugar. One chopped shallot or a little onion, a scrape of dried horseradish, a small pinch of pimento and of crushed chopped bay leaf, one leaf of rosemary. This takes several months but is worth it! If you find this vinegar a little strong, then divide the contents of the first bottle into another.

Garlic Vinegar — The old recipe says that this is best made between Midsummer and Michaelmas, but that was before we could import garlic so easily. Some do not like the smell or flavour. I like both and believe it helps bring out most savoury flavours. Garlic is said to be good for you — never mind what the others say! Peel, chop and add one ounce of fresh garlic. Shake the bottle each day for ten days, then strain and re-bottle. You need use only a few drops at a time.

Horseradish and Chilli Vinegar — A powerful one, this! Use one ounce of grated horseradish, a teaspoonful of sea salt, a saltspoon of dried ginger root, a pinch of cayenne pepper and a whole hot chilli.

Nasturtium Vinegar — Quite a piquant and unusual flavour comes from using a handful of freshly gathered nasturtium flowers, one clove, two peppercorns, a hint of crushed garlic and one chopped shallot (or a little onion). This is best kept for a month or two before using.

Rosemary Vinegar (Italian style) — Use a large sprig each of rosemary and of peppermint, together with a half teaspoon of chopped angelica root.

Shallot Vinegar — Use four ounces of chopped

shallots. A large onion will do instead but the flavour is not as good.

Spiced Vinegar — In this case the spices need to be simmered with a very little of the vinegar. This is then added when cool to the rest and allowed to mature for a week. It is best then sieved and re-bottled. Use half a teaspoon each of crushed chillies, pimento and coriander with a quarter teaspoon each of cloves, ginger root, mustard powder and black pepper.

Tarragon Vinegar — Known to the French as *estragon*, tarragon is perhaps the most French of all herbs. It is strong, so you do not need to use much. Without doubt tarragon is the best herb to go with chicken but as tarragon vinegar it is used in the finest French dressings. Put a few fresh branches into the vinegar and it is soon ready for use. In this instance it is never a good idea to remove the tarragon as the vinegar drains away as you pour it. If you have no tarragon in your garden grow the variety called True French. Russian tarragon is rather less good.

SALAD DRESSINGS

There are not many attractive undressed things and salads are no exception. The variety you can use is a delight to the palate. The cook has the pleasure of deciding which will suit both the guests and the salad.

I find olive oil has a rather heavy and dominating flavour which does not attract me, but you may certainly use it if you like it. Use a first pressing olive oil in that case. Otherwise you will note that I have listed corn oil. This is because it is a good, moderately priced oil without much tendency to rancidity. It has a high content of the valuable unsaturated fats. You can equally well substitute corn oil by soya, safflower or sunflower oils.

Basic French Dressing

> 3 parts corn oil
> 1 part cider vinegar

Mix and add to the salad just before serving so that every leaf is shining. Many French people would use 6 parts oil to 1 part cider vinegar but that is too oily for my taste.

Tarragon Dressing

As above, using tarragon cider vinegar instead of the plain sort.

My Favourite Dressing

We have evolved this which our guests seem to like – it took a long time to get it right.

At least an hour before the meal (or the day before if you wish) mix:

> 3 tablespoons corn oil
> 1 tablespoon cider vinegar
> a squeeze of lemon juice
> one large crushed clove of garlic
> a turn of freshly ground black pepper
> a pinch of raw sugar
> a pinch of mustard powder
> some mixed herbs (see below)

Add to the salad after a brisk mix either at table or just before serving. Never use so much that there is a lot of free dressing at the bottom of the salad bowl.

For the mixed herbs I keep two assortments of dried herbs in screw-topped jars. They are slightly different from each other. I use whichever I happen to fancy. They are:

Herb Mix (A)— Parsley, tarragon, lemon balm, chervil, chives, dill, thyme, basil.

Herb Mix (B)— Parsley, dill, celery leaf flakes and tarragon.

The herbs are listed in roughly descending order of quantity, first largest, last least.

Yogurt Salad Dressing

This is good as it comes or can have herbs or garlic added as you wish. Blend or whisk thoroughly:

> 1 small carton of plain yogurt then,
> using the carton as a measure
> half a carton cider vinegar
> half a carton corn oil

Vinaigrette Dressings

These come in a wonderful assortment of flavours. The basic dressing is:

> 6 tablespoons corn oil
> 2 tablespoons cider vinegar
> 1 teaspoon chopped capers
> 1 tablespoon chopped onion
> 1 tablespoon herbs in the mixture, 2 parts
> parsley to one each of chervil, tarragon
> and chives
> a pinch of sea salt and pepper

Mix thoroughly. Use with avocado pears, asparagus, cauliflowers, game, meat or salad.

The quantities can be halved or doubled, as required.

Vinaigrette with Eggs
There are two good ways of doing this, the first is best for chicken and fish, the second with salads.

Recipe (A)— Soft boil 2 eggs (3 minutes) Scoop out the yolks, add these to the basic dressing and mix. Chop the white, stir it gently in.

Recipe (B)— Use 2 hard-boiled chopped eggs, a little chopped gherkin and a little chopped lemon peel with the basic dressing. Stir gently.

Curried Vinaigrette
Add a teaspoonful of curry powder and an extra-finely chopped onion to the basic dressing. Allow to stand several hours before use.

Blue Cheese Dressing
Add from one to four tablespoonsful of crumbled dry Roquefort, Stilton, Danish Blue or Gorgonzola.

Nutty Salad Dressing
This is rather good with cold rice, or with

chicory and other full-flavoured salads.

> 2 tablespoons cider vinegar
> 1 tablespoon corn oil
> ¼ teaspoon mustard powder
> 1 saltspoon mixed herbs (see above)
> 1 egg yolk (raw)
> 1 tablespoon mixed coarsely chopped nuts
> 1 small chopped apple

You need to add the nuts and apple after the other ingredients have been thoroughly beaten together. If you find the dressing a little sharp you can add a touch of honey or of raw sugar to taste.

Banana Dressing

Unusual but an interesting change especially with chicory.

> 2 tablespoons cider vinegar
> 1 tablespoon corn oil
> 1 tablespoon natural yogurt
> a pinch of sea salt and pepper
> a big pinch of mixed herbs
> banana (1 or more depending on the number of people)

Crush the banana with a fork until it becomes smooth and creamy. Mix well in firstly the yogurt, then the herbs. Next add the cider vinegar and the oil. Mix very briskly. Finely chopped ham is a good addition if you like it.

I am sure you will enjoy these cider vinegar dressings and have pleasure discovering and trying many others.

SAUCES

At home we enjoy the extra fullness of flavour
and delicate aroma which comes from using
cider vinegar in our sauces. Some of the old,
traditional recipes are particularly interesting
and much enjoyed. A few new ideas bring excitement — but first one of the basic sauces which,
although from simple ingredients, requires a
little care for good results:

Sauce Hollandaise

This is best made 'finger-tip hot' or just as
hot as the finger-tip will stand. Over-heating
will produce bad scrambled egg. Take:

    8 ounces butter
    4 egg yolks
    1 tablespoonful cider vinegar
    a pinch of sea salt and freshly ground pepper
    1 tablespoonful cold water

Boil a large saucepan about one-third full of
water. While it is heating, cut the butter into
some twenty small pieces. Put the water,
cider vinegar and the egg yolks into a small
enamel or stainless steel saucepan, whisk in
the salt and pepper whilst continuing to
whisk, gently lower the pan into the boiling
water. As soon as the yolks become thicker,
take the pan from the water, put in one of
the pats of butter. Whisk again to a smooth
cream, add another pat of butter. If it melts
whisk again to a cream. Go on until the
butter does not melt. Return the pan to the
water until it just melts. Do not stop
beating. Do this until all the butter has been

used. When this has happened again warm up the sauce, still beating, until it is finger-tip hot. Serve immediately in a warm sauce-boat.

I like this on the huge tender asparagus spears, beloved of the Germans, which are eatable from tip to base — but Hollandaise is good with many vegetables.

I hope you have not become discouraged by the difficulties of that one, but the sauces become easier from now on!

Aïoli Sauce

If you believe that garlic is good for you, this sauce is a way of making sure everyone knows. It is made to the consistency of mayonnaise. In Marseille they call it 'Friday Sauce' because it is used on fish. We like it with boiled potatoes, French beans and hard-boiled eggs, as well.

    4 cloves garlic (or 2 for each person)
    2 egg yolks (or 1 each)
    8 fluid ounces corn oil
    sea salt, pepper, cider vinegar

Either crush the garlic to a paste or put it in a blender with the egg yolks and salt. Add the oil *very* gradually, whisking or blending all the time. Stop when you have made a thick mayonnaise. Add pepper and cider vinegar to taste. We use about a tablespoon of the vinegar. Lord Burntwood tells me that Aïoli was created because of the need to disguise the strong salted fish brought to

France by the Newfoundland fishing boats
from the eighteenth-century onwards.

Mayonnaise
It is possible nowadays to buy ready-made
mayonnaise containing cider vinegar, sunflower oil and fresh egg yolks. This is as
good as home made, but here is how to do it
yourself.

    3 egg yolks
    ½ teaspoonful sea salt
    ½ teaspoonful mustard powder
    1 tablespoon boiling water
    10 fluid ounces corn or sunflower seed oil
    1 tablespoon cider vinegar
    (*Tarragon* cider vinegar is best)

Have all the ingredients and the bowl at
room temperature. Put egg yolks into the
bowl and beat for about a minute until they
thicken. Add the cider vinegar, sea salt and
mustard. Beat for one more minute. Keep
beating steadily and then add the oil a drop
at a time. If you go too fast it will curdle. (If
that happens start again with another yolk
and a little oil and add this to the failure to
revive it.) As you add more oil it will
become easier. After almost a half has been
combined, you can increase the oil to a thin
stream. When the oil has been used, beat in a
tablespoonful of boiling water. This helps to
prevent it separating. Taste to see if you
have enough seasoning. Many people find
that they prefer two or three tablespoons of
cider vinegar. If you do this in the blender

you need 1 whole egg and 2 yolks.

Having made your mayonnaise, or bought it, you can try lots of good variations.

Louis Sauce (for shellfish)

    6 fluid ounces (about 1 cup) mayonnaise
    2 tablespoons grated onion
    2 fluid ounces chilli sauce (see separate recipe)
    2 tablespoons chopped parsley
    3 fluid ounces whipped double cream
    a dash of cayenne

Stir together. Allow to stand for about two hours in a cool place to develop the flavour.

Ravigote Sauce (one of the best for cold vegetables or shellfish)

    6 fluid ounces mayonnaise
    1 tablespoon cider vinegar
    1 teaspoon mustard powder
    1 chopped shallot
    1 tablespoon chopped capers
    1 teaspoon chopped tarragon

Mix gently. Serve cold.

Thousand Island (the best for prawn cocktail)

    6 fluid ounces mayonnaise
    1 dash Tabasco sauce or
    1 tablespoon chilli sauce
    1 tablespoon cider vinegar
    4 tablespoons tomato purée (from a tube is easy)

Stir together and chill before use.

Tartare Sauce

    6 fluid ounces mayonnaise
    1 chopped hard-boiled egg yolk
    1 medium grated onion

1 tablespoon chopped chives
1 teaspoon fine chopped parsley
1 tablespoon chopped capers
2 teaspoons cider vinegar

Mix well and allow to stand an hour before using.

Mayonnaise Chantilly

6 fluid ounces mayonnaise
2 fluid ounces whipped cream

Stir the two gently together.

You can invent your own. Amongst tried favourites are mayonnaise with any of the following for 6 fluid ounces:

Asparagus, 2 oz. chopped, drained.

Chives, 1 tablespoonful chopped

Curry powder, 2 teaspoonsful (best if cooked before adding with a little oil and onion)

Cheese (add 3 tablespoons grated cheese and some paprika, thin with cream)

Chutney (drain first)

Chilli powder (not too much, ¼ teaspoon to try)

Green (coloured with juice crushed from 4 tablespoons watercress, 2 tablespoons parsley)

Mustard (add 2 tablespoonsful mustard powder)

Paprika, 1 teaspoonful (very pretty rose colour)

Verte (pound up 1 teaspoonful chives, 1 tablespoonful chervil, 1 tablespoonful tarragon, 1 tablespoonful spinach with 1 tablespoonful water. Squeeze through muslin into mayonnaise.)

Sauce Béarnaise

This king of French sauces, surely the best accompaniment to steak, was accidently left out of my first draft of this book. Thankfully Lord Burntwood noted the omission of this favourite of his before it was too late!

2 tablespoonsful cider vinegar
1 teaspoonful chopped shallots (or onions)
6 peppercorns
A bay leaf
2 teaspoons tarragon
2 teaspoons chervil
¼ cup (approximately) gravy or stock
1½ ounces butter
2 egg yolks

First of all you boil up the shallots and peppercorns, bay leaf, and half of the chervil and tarragon in the cider vinegar until it has reduced to half. Strain and reserve the liquid. Put a double saucepan on and boil it fast (a basin in an ordinary saucepan will do if you give it time to heat through). Mix the egg yolks with a little of the stock and put in the double boiler, stirring constantly. Still stirring, add the butter, a small piece at a time. When the mixture has thickened, add the rest of the stock and then the cider vinegar liquor. Finally, stir in the rest of the chervil and tarragon and serve piping hot.

Chilli Sauce
This is very hot, but marvellous in small amounts or as an addition to other sauces.

6 hot red chillies, chopped finely, including seeds
4 large onions, chopped very fine
3 lbs. peeled tomatoes
6 tablespoonsful raw sugar
3 tablespoonsful sea salt
25 fluid ounces (1¼ pints) cider vinegar

Boil gently for an hour, stirring frequently. Pour into warm jars. Seal.

Cole Slaw Sauce (for use with white raw shredded cabbage)
Here are two recipes for this delicious sauce, the first more suitable for general use, the second for a special occasion.

Standard

Dissolve 2 ounces butter over a low heat, add 1 tablespoon flour (81 per cent. wholemeal). Slowly add 4 fluid ounces water, stirring all the time, to make a cream. Cook until smooth and quite thick. Beat 2 eggs, 2 tablespoonsful raw sugar, 1 teaspoonful mustard powder and a pinch of sea salt in a bowl. Then pour over hot mixture, stirring constantly. Return the lot to the *low* heat. As soon as it thickens, take off heat. Add 4 fluid ounces cider vinegar. Cool before using.

Special

  6 egg yolks
  1 tablespoon butter
  1 teaspoon mustard powder
  2 tablespoons raw sugar (light coloured)
  8 fluid ounces cider vinegar
  juice of one lemon
  5 fluid ounces double cream, whipped

Beat the eggs over water (see *Hollandaise* recipe). When they lighten in colour add everything except lemon juice and cream. Beat over heat until thick, add lemon juice and beat again. When cold stir in the cream.

Mint Sauces

Take a large enough bunch of mint, wash clean, take off the leaves, chop fine (we use a cheap gadget of French origin). Add, for four people, one teaspoonful raw sugar, cover with cider vinegar. Leave for at least half-an-hour before using.

We like also mint jelly. To do that add 1 tablespoonful gelatine crystals to 4 fluid ounces hot cider vinegar. When dissolved, add 4 fluid ounces cold cider vinegar together with raw sugar and mint as above.

Poivrade Sauce (hot, for meats and vegetarian roasts)

> 1 large chopped onion
> 2 grated carrots
> 3 tablespoonsful chopped parsley
> 2 tablespoonsful corn oil
> ½ bay leaf
> pinch thyme

Cook together for five minutes or so.

Add: 5 fluid ounces red wine

3 tablespoonsful cider vinegar

Cook until reduced to half.

Add: 12 fluid ounces thick brown gravy.

Cook for half-an-hour. Strain into clean saucepan with a pinch of ground cloves and 2 teaspoonsful freshly ground black pepper. Stir well and cook gently for five minutes more.

Sorrel Sauce

A traditional accompaniment to vegetables.

This recipe is seventeenth-century.

Crush about 3 ounces of chopped sorrel with the flesh of two peeled eating apples. Beat in a teaspoon of raw sugar and a tablespoon of cider vinegar. No need to cook this one!

Sweet and Sour Sauce (Beloved of the Chinese and good with many fried things and undercooked vegetables.)

- 8 tablespoons cider vinegar
- 8 tablespoons honey
- 1 small green pepper (sweet) chopped fine
- 1 tablespoon chopped almonds

Mix and heat gently before serving. You can also add a clove of crushed garlic. If you prefer a milder sweet and sour sauce, add up to half-a-pint of stock to taste.

Worcestershire Sauce

Most recipes for this famous sauce contain a lot of anchovies, which are not to every taste. Here is a well-tried method, too extravagant for the commercial producer. A cheap sherry, preferably dry, is good enough.

- 2 teaspoons pimento
- 1 teaspoon clove
- 1 teaspoon black pepper
- 1 teaspoon ginger
- 1 teaspoon chilli powder
- 1 ounce curry powder
- 2 ounces mustard
- 2 ounces bruised shallots
- 2 ounces sea salt

    8 ounces raw sugar (dark)
    4 ounces tamarinds
    1 pint sherry
    2 pints cider vinegar
    a touch of caramel to colour

Use whole spices where available. Bruise them by roughly pounding. Simmer everything, except the sherry, together for an hour. Top up with more cider vinegar if any has been lost by evaporation. Add the sherry and any colour needed (caramel). Leave for a week. Coarsely strain and bottle.

CHUTNEY, PICKLES AND MUSTARDS

You can substitute cider vinegar for ordinary vinegar in any recipe, but here are some tested and occasionally unusual ways of making these excellent accompaniments.

Apple Chutney (An old Devon recipe)

    40 fluid ounces cider vinegar
    2 lb. apples (cored and peeled)
    1 lb. raw sugar
    1 lb. raisins (seedless)
    2 teaspoonsful sea salt
    1 lb. onions
    1 ounce mustard powder
    1 teaspoonful cayenne pepper

Chop all ingredients coarsely. Boil until tender, about one hour. Pour into hot jars. Seal.

Apple and Blackberry Chutney (another Devon treat)

    1½ lb. apples (cored and peeled)

1½ lb. blackberries
10 fluid ounces cider vinegar
½ lb. raw sugar
1 teaspoonful sea salt
4 ounces raisins (seedless)
4 ounces sultanas
2 cloves crushed garlic *or*
3 small chopped onions
1 teaspoonful ground ginger

Crush the blackberries in the pan with the vinegar. Simmer for twenty minutes and rub through a coarse sieve (I use a colander). Add the other ingredients. Cook gently until thick, this takes about forty minutes. Pour into hot jars and seal.

Green Tomato Chutney

This recipe was devised by Martlet. None of my garden-grown tomatoes ripened one year so we tried this recipe and found it very good.

4 lb. green tomatoes
1½ lb. onions
1½ lb. apples (after peeling and coring)
1 lb. sultanas
2 lb. raw sugar
2 ounces mustard powder
4 ounces sea salt
1 ounce ground ginger
1 ounce crushed garlic
1 teaspoonful cayenne pepper
juice of 2 lemons
2½ pints cider vinegar

Slice the tomatoes, apples and onions thinly. Mix well with the other ingredients. Simmer for 2 hours or until well cooked and thick.

Bengal Apple Chutney

This is highly spiced and a first-rate accompaniment to curries and savouries.

    3 pints cider vinegar
    1 lb. raw sugar
    2 ounces mustard seed
    8 ounces raisins (seedless)
    2 ounces garlic
    8 ounces onions
    7 lb. cooking apples
    2 tablespoonsful sea salt
    ½ ounce chilli powder
    1 teaspoonful cumin powder (if available)
    2 ounces fresh ginger *or*
    4 teaspoonsful powdered ginger

Scrape the ginger, but mind the eyes whilst you do it! Mince it with the onions and garlic. Core, slice and peel the apples. Simmer the apples with the cider vinegar and raw sugar until the apples are quite soft. Add everything else and simmer for another twenty minutes, stirring frequently. Bottle.

Tomato Ketchup

Ketchup is a modern word for a thin chutney. In about 1690 it was called *catchup*. In the 1730s the name became *catsup*, which is often still used in America. Only in the last century was ketchup made commonly with tomatoes. Before then, walnuts and mushrooms were the usual basis.

    3 lb. tomatoes
    2 ounces sea salt
    1 pint cider vinegar

2 ounces raw sugar
2 teaspoonsful mustard powder
1 teaspoonful pepper

Peel the tomatoes by plunging them first into boiling water for a second. Chop them coarsely, sprinkle with the sea salt and allow to stand for at least 3 hours. Boil with the other ingredients for half an hour, stirring frequently until thick and smooth. Fill into clean bottles whilst still hot. Keep for a few days before using.

Hot Peach Chutney

This is best made with slightly unripe peaches. If you do not want it hot, replace the chilli and ginger by a teaspoon of mustard powder and ¼ teaspoon of pepper.

2 lb. peaches
1 lb. raw sugar
1 pint cider vinegar
8 ounces sultanas
1 ounce chilli powder
1 teaspoonful ginger powder

Skin the peaches. Halve them and remove the stones. Bring half the cider vinegar to the boil with the raw sugar. Lower the halved peaches into the liquid. Simmer until they are soft. Add all the remaining ingredients. Simmer until thick. Bottle. This is best matured for a few weeks to bring out the flavour. The recipe is worth trying with plums. These do not need peeling.

Pickled Onions
In olden times you used a silver knife for
peeling the onions as steel discolours the
flesh. Today stainless steel is fine. We like
our onions crisp. If you prefer yours softer
then cook them for 5-7 minutes in the
spiced vinegar before bottling.

After you have peeled the onions, cover
them with water to which has been added 3
ounces sea salt for every pint. As the onions
like to float, I put a plate on top to keep
them down. Leave the onions for at least
twenty-four hours — forty-eight hours or
longer does no harm — before thoroughly
draining them.

Spiced Vinegar is best made at the same time
as you brine the onions. You can buy ready
mixed pickling spice which is very good, but
if you prefer to make your own use, to every
quart (40 fluid ounces) of vinegar: ¼ ounce
allspice, ¼ ounce blade mace, ¼ ounce
cinnamon sticks, 20 peppercorns and, if
liked, ¼ ounce root ginger in the piece, plus
four or five whole dried red chillies. You can
either tie the spices in a bag of muslin (in
which case add ¼ ounce cloves) or you can,
as we do, bottle the spices with the onions.
The first way looks best. We prefer the
flavour the second way. In either case,
simmer the spices in the vinegar for an hour,
with the lid on a stainless steel saucepan, and
leave to cool and mature until the onions are

ready for bottling. Pack the dry onions carefully into sterile jars (leave the empty jars for an hour in the oven on gas mark 1 or electric 275° (F) and allow to cool). Pour on the spiced vinegar and store in a cool place.

This method works also with cauliflower, green tomatoes and cucumbers.

Piccalilli

>   3 lb. green tomatoes
>   ½ lb. cabbage
>   1 lb. cauliflower florets
>   1 large cucumber
>   4 medium onions *plus*
>   20 pickling onions if available
>   2 tablespoonsful sea salt
>   2 pints cider vinegar
>   1 lb. raw sugar
>   3 teaspoonsful turmeric
>   4 ounces mustard powder
>   1 teaspoonful black pepper
>   2 ounces tapioca starch or,
>   if not available, cornflour

Mix the tapioca powder or cornflour in a little cider vinegar then simmer the rest of the ingredients for fifteen minutes. Turn off the heat, add the cider vinegar/tapioca or starch mixture and allow to cool. Chop all the vegetables and place in layers in basins with layers of sea salt between. Let this stay overnight. Drain off the liquid completely. Mix the sauce and the vegetables thoroughly. Put into sterile jars, seal carefully. Ready for use in two weeks.

Pickled Eggs
Cider vinegar has the special property of preventing discolouration of the eggs. All you have to do is to gently boil the eggs for twenty minutes, shell them while still quite hot and drop them straight into cider vinegar in a storage jar.

Pickled Sausages
Lovely for picnics, especially if you can obtain your sausages from a reliable butcher who avoids extenders, binders, emulsifiers and the like.

Deep fry the sausages in corn oil until well-done. Drop them straight into cider vinegar. They will keep for months in a cool place.

Rollmops
Soak herring fillets in brine, just as for pickled onions, with 3 ounces sea salt to each pint of water, but with the addition of 2 tablespoons of cider vinegar to each pint. Leave them for four hours in a cool place. Then replace the brine with cider vinegar with 1 ounce sea salt per pint, and leave for a further twelve hours. Finally wrap each fillet round some shredded onion and fasten the tail with a cocktail stick. Put in fresh cider vinegar with some herbs or spices, especially paprika and bay leaves, if you like. They will keep for four weeks or much longer in the fridge.

Mackerel in Vinegar
Fillet the fish. Dry them by dredging with
flour. Fry in corn oil until golden. Leave to
cool. Put a layer of the fish into a bowl,
sprinkle with sea salt and raw sugar then
another layer of fish and so on until all is
used. Slice an onion thickly, put this over
the top layer, sprinkle with pepper. Cover
with cider vinegar. Leave in a cool place for
two or three days. Taste the vinegar adding
more raw sugar if required. This keeps for
weeks in a cool place.

English Mustard
Instead of mixing powdered mustard with
water, use cider vinegar. Allow the mixture
to stand for about half-an-hour to develop
the flavour. Mustard tastes better and keeps
longer this way.

German Mustard
Take 2 ounces mustard powder with 1 ounce
cornflour or tapioca flour. Mix in a large
pinch each of ginger powder, ground cloves,
ground carraway seeds, a teaspoon of sea salt
and two of raw sugar. Make the lot into a
fairly thick mustard by gently cooking it
with half a pint of cider vinegar. Allow to
cool and store in small sealed pots.

DRINKS
There are some old ways of using cider vinegar
as an essential ingredient for a refreshing
summer drink.

Cowslip Cider Vinegar

Collect a quarter of a pound of cowslip 'pips', as the flowers are called, pull them from the stalks, cover with a pint of cider vinegar and allow to marinade for three days. Strain the liquor through a fine sieve or some muslin into a stainless steel or enamelled saucepan. Add 1 lb. of raw sugar and stir until dissolved. Put the lid on and stand the pan in a larger pan of boiling water. Cook like this for an hour, topping up the water, as necessary. Bottle when cold. It is better if you add a wineglass of brandy to each pint! Dilute with soda or ice cold water, as required.

Elderflower Sparkling Wine

You will need 2 heads elderflowers in full bloom, 1 lemon, 2 tablespoonsful cider vinegar, 1 gallon cold water and 1½ lb. raw sugar.

Squeeze the lemon and put with the quartered peel into a non-metal container. Add the other ingredients and leave for twenty-four hours. Strain and pour into clean, screw-top bottles. Keep for at least two weeks before using.

Fruit Cider Vinegars

Many people in olden times thought a drink of a diluted fruit cider vinegar was a good winter health promoter. You may like to try the idea. You can use any soft fruit, raspberries and blackcurrants being especially nice. You can use up the small or squashed fruits very well this way. Use one pint of cider vinegar to each pound of fruit. Mix the cider vinegar and fruit together and stir them from time to time for about five days. Strain the liquid, pressing out as much as possible from the fruit pulp. Add half-a-pound, or more to taste, or light raw sugar to each pint. Boil for ten minutes and fill into warmed bottles, whilst still hot.

You can use these vinegars as interesting varieties for dressings but they are excellent as a drink, when you may wish to add extra sugar.

SOME OTHER IDEAS
Cheese Softening
In 1577, a certain B. Goodge wrote these words, 'Hard cheese wrapped in cloutes wet in cyder vinegar returnes to a softness'.

Stopping Potatoes Browning
Add a good splash of cider vinegar to the water into which you slice potatoes. When you have finished you can dry them, prior to frying, with far less chance of their going brown.

Steaming Vegetables
When you cook vegetables by the healthy method of steaming them (there is less vitamin and mineral loss this way), add 2

teaspoonsful of cider vinegar to the water you use. This helps the vegetables keep their colour without the vitamin C depleting effect that comes from using bicarbonate of soda.

Poached Eggs

I do not care for those moulded eggs which come from bought egg poachers. They seem to lack interest and excitement. I put a saucepan of water on to boil, add two teaspoonsful of cider vinegar and wait until it is simmering gently. Meanwhile I have cracked one or two eggs into a small container or cup which is less than half the width of the pan. With a wooden spoon I briskly stir the bubbling liquid. When it is going smoothly, I gently pour the eggs into the vortex of the little whirlpool that has been created. The whites coagulate nicely and in two minutes I am ready to serve the poached eggs upon wholemeal toast.

Furniture Polish

This is not a joke! Nor have I substituted cider vinegar in a recipe usually using the ordinary type. The formula, as it stands, is the recommendation of the United States Bureau of Standards.

Cider vinegar	12½ pounds
Petroleum spirits	22½ pounds
Turpentine	13½ pounds
Denatured alcohol	2¼ pounds
Boiled linseed oil	10 pounds

Raw linseed oil   12 pounds

These quantities produce 10 gallons of polish which should *not* be stored in metal containers because these may be corroded by the cider vinegar. You can use ounces instead of pounds for a smaller quantity of this very economical and good quality polish.

SAVOURY DISHES

My family loves the added aroma and softness cider vinegar gives to so many dishes. Here are a few you may like trying — our tastes embrace many ways of eating so keep on tasting until the dish suits you. I am sure there are many folk tales in cookery, one of them is flaming a dish in brandy. This expensive waste can be replaced by a quarter of the brandy, not flamed, added just before you serve. Sometimes a dash of angostura bitters does instead, this is especially good in soups. To start with a real scorcher:

Vindaloo Chicken
You require:
    1 3 lb. chicken
    1 teaspoonful mustard powder
    2 teaspoonsful chilli powder
    2 teaspoonsful cumin powder
    6 cloves
    6 cloves of garlic (unless you are frightened)
    2 teaspoonsful turmeric (sold in Indian shops)
    1 teaspoonful ginger
    1 stick cinnamon
    1 tablespoonful raw sugar

    2 teaspoonsful sea salt
    3 tablespoonsful corn oil
    3 tablespoonsful cider vinegar
    2 large onion

Take all the ingredients except the chicken,
onion and oil, mix them to a pulp, crushing
the garlic and cloves. Cut up the chicken,
cover all parts with the mixture. Leave for at
least five hours, a day is better, in a cool
place. Fry the onion in the corn oil. Add the
chicken and spices. Cook in a closed saucepan until the chicken is cooked through. I
like an extra sprinkle of cumin just before
serving.

Vindaloo Vegetables

The foregoing recipe can also be used with
certain vegetables, either a mixture or, more
successfully, courgettes, aubergines, mushrooms and sweet peppers.

Barbecued Spare Ribs of Pork

Cheap and lovely. If you do not have a
barbecue, use a medium grill to finish off.
The recipe will do for four pounds of spare
ribs. Take:

    4 tablespoonsful sherry
    1¼ pint white stock (or a good cube)
    1 tablespoonful honey
    2 tablespoonsful cider vinegar
    1 tablespoonful soya sauce
    1 tablespoonful raw sugar
    1 teaspoonful ginger powder
    2 cloves crushed garlic

Mix all the ingredients. Cut up the spare ribs,

marinade for twenty-four hours in a cool place. Take out the ribs and roast in a pan at 350°(F) or Mark 5. Drain off fat, finish on barbecue or under grill, basting with marinade, until crisp.

Rice Salad
You can use mushrooms or prawns instead of the anchovy fillets, if you prefer. Take:
    ½ lb. rice (basmati is best;
    patna almost as good)
    2 ounce tin anchovy fillets
    4 ounces olives (stoned: black are best)
    3 tablespoonsful corn oil
    1 tablespoonful cider vinegar,
       sea salt, pepper
    1 sliced tomato
    1 cup cooked green peas
Cook the rice in lots of boiling, sea salted water. After ten minutes fish out a grain and test it for softness with your finger nails. Do this again each minute until the rice has softened moderately. Drain the rice through a sieve, wash with cold running water. Drain completely, put in a basin until cold. Add the other ingredients having mixed the oil, cider vinegar, pepper and sea salt. Stir gently until completely mixed. Decorate with a sliced green pepper or tomato.

Shashlik
Take and cut into large cubes enough lean, tender lamb for your needs. Put the lamb to marinade for about half a day in enough

cider vinegar to cover, with lots of raw onion rings.

Skewer the cubes. You can, if you wish, alternate the lamb with green peppers, bacon and sliced tomatoes. Brush with corn oil and grill on a hot flame until done. Serve with the onion rings from the cider vinegar, sprinkle with cumin seed and perhaps a little salt and paprika.

Pork Chops in Tomato

    6 pork chops
    1 cup cider vinegar
    1 cup stock (or beef stock cube)
    1 tablespoonful corn oil
    4 tablespoonsful tomato paste

Trim fat from chops and seal quickly in hot corn oil. Pour off any fat in the pan, add the cider vinegar. Cover pan and simmer, turning chops from time to time. When the cider vinegar has greatly reduced, add the other ingredients and cook for half-an-hour more. If the sauce is too thick, add more water.

Mexican Hot Pot

Brown 1 lb. diced stewing steak with 2 large, sliced onions. Add 1 teaspoonful chilli powder, 1 teaspoonful sea salt, 1 tablespoonful cider vinegar, 1 cup water or stock. Cook gently in the oven for two hours. If you like, add haricot beans before cooking, in which case add extra water.

Partridge in Chocolate

An exotic and delicious Spanish dish. Chicken will do as an alternative. You will need:

    1 partridge
    1 cup boiling water
    1 large chopped onion
    3 tablespoonsful cider vinegar
    1 tablespoonful parsley
    3 cloves garlic
    corn oil
    2 tablespoonsful grated plain chocolate
    1 tablespoonful wholemeal breadcrumbs

Brown the bird in a casserole with the hot oil. Add the garlic, parsley and chopped onion and brown them lightly. Then put in the cider vinegar and boiling water. Stew gently in the oven until cooked then increase heat, add the chocolate and breadcrumbs and boil for a few minutes before serving.

Almond and Garlic Soup with Grapes

Another Spanish recipe, from Malaga where the grapes are sweet. There they use freshly shelled almonds dried slightly in the oven and then powdered. We use the less beautiful shop-bought ground almonds, but the soup is an interesting summer starter.

    2 tablespoonsful ground almonds
    6 cloves garlic
    2 tablespoonsful corn oil
    1 pint water
    1½ tablespoonsful cider vinegar
    8 ice cubes
    2 teaspoonsful sea salt

> 1 lb. skinned, seeded grapes
> ½ cup wholemeal breadcrumbs

Pound together with garlic, almonds, salt and oil until smooth. Add the cider vinegar, grapes, water and ice cubes. Leave one hour in a cold place before serving.

Gazpacho Soup

This most famous Spanish cold soup comes from Andalusia. You can either pound the solid ingredients together, apart from the cucumber, then add the oil drop by drop until it becomes thick when you stir in the cider vinegar and add the cucumber; or you can save trouble by using a blender to do your initial blend, adding the oil whilst still blending. If it is too thick, add some water. Add the ice. Chill before serving and garnish with chopped parsley or chives. You need:

> 5 tomatoes
> 4 cloves garlic
> ½ cup cider vinegar
> 1 chopped onion
> sea salt and pepper
> ½ a cucumber, finely chopped
> 1 cup wholemeal breadcrumbs
> 1 sweet red pepper, chopped
> 8 ice cubes

Cold Potatoes

An excellent accompaniment for savouries of all sorts.

> 1½ lb. small new potatoes (unpeeled)
> 2 ounces streaky bacon
> 2 tablespoonsful cider vinegar
> 2 tablespoonsful chopped chives or onion

Cut the potatoes into pieces and sprinkle with the chives or onion. Sprinkle with sea salt and pepper. Dice the fat bacon and cook it in its own fat until crisp. Add the vinegar very carefully because it foams. Pour over the potatoes and serve when cold.

Boiled Salmon

I find that this way does just as well for lobster which takes twenty minutes in the boiling liquor. Salmon takes about thirty minutes, then you let it cool, in the fridge, in the juice. This makes the salmon very moist and it will keep for a day or so if needed.

Slice 2 onions, 2 carrots and a leek if you have it into ¼ pint of cider vinegar, plus half-a-pint of white wine, or water will do. Add 3 pints of water, a large handful of parsley with about a third as much thyme and two bay leaves. Grind in some black pepper. Bring to the boil and simmer gently for an hour. Put in the salmon and simmer until done. It is often easier to lower and raise the fish on a piece of muslin.

Cacik (Turkish Cucumber Soup)

You need for this very nice cold soup (which might have been invented by a health food cook):

    1 peeled halved and seeded cucumber
    3 x 5 ounce cartons plain yogurt

2 teaspoonsful cider vinegar
1 small teaspoonful corn oil
milk
2 teaspoonsful chopped mint

Grate the cucumber and blend it with the yogurt (or put them in a liquidizer). Season to taste, add the oil and cider vinegar. Mix well, then thin to the required consistency with cold milk.

Chill well and just before serving put into cold bowls and sprinkle with the chopped mint.

CHAPTER SIX

CIDER VINEGAR IN THE TREATMENT OF ANIMALS

As I have implied, this section is the key to the whole cider vinegar system of treatment. The allergy specialist, Dr. Erik Andersson, who had many reports of the effective use of cider vinegar, honey and beeswax among his patients, said that it has become a rule of thumb in tests which include placebos (that is, treatments using an ingredient which the patient believes is the one that will work, whereas an inert alternative is used instead) that up to a third of the placebo group frequently feels an improvement.

What we humans experience when we are ill is often reduced, aggravated or maybe even caused by our mental processes. I have no reason to believe that cows, pigs, sheep and horses fall into this psychologically motivated category. Yet cider vinegar works very regularly in some common animal complaints. It is used regularly by farmers who certainly cannot afford to waste money on an outside chance of improvement.

This gives me good reason to believe that the remarkable results observed from the use of cider vinegar in man are not just faith healing but are a real and positive contribution to sound health.

Many theories have been proposed as to why cider vinegar works and it may be that there is not one answer but several. More research is required and is, I know, being undertaken in certain areas of study, such as asthma. A most interesting and exciting recent observation was that one of the causative organisms of mastitis in the cow, *Streptococcus mammitis*, when grown in the laboratory, is killed by the application of a small amount of cider vinegar. In response to my enquiries, the chemist told me that neither ordinary vinegar of the same acidity nor cider itself had this effect. Here then is a piece of concrete evidence that there is something very special about cider vinegar. In this connexion, the suggestion has been made that the natural balance of phenols and tannins in the acetic cider vinegar is not all that different from the basic chemical materials from which scientists produce bacteria-destroying drugs. The thought this raises is the profound idea that through the use of cider vinegar you enable the body to produce within itself valuable substances for its own protection. It will take many years to test the truth of this proposition, but it is a most provoking suggestion.

Dr. D.C. Jarvis was the first to systematically investigate the effects of cider vinegar on large groups of cattle. He considered that it helped to maintain a correct balance between the acids and alkalis in the animal's body chemistry. He found this to be of crucial importance in building up resistance to many common farmyard illnesses. At first he thought that the potassium content was the effective factor, so he carried out experiments which showed that the cider vinegar had a good effect not obtained from the use of potassium alone. I shall deal with some of the most usual successful uses of cider vinegar in animal treatment. Although the animals are dealt with individually, the experience of one is often applicable to another. It is therefore worth looking for any condition not specifically considered in the section devoted to other animals.

FOR CATTLE

Unquestionably the greatest agricultural use for cider vinegar is in the treatment and prevention of common ailments amongst cattle and for improving general condition, milk yield and fertility.

The usual dose for adult animals is about four fluid ounces per day which may be given as just over two tablespoonsful, twice a day.

If the animal is suffering from poor appetite, the cider vinegar can be used as a drench with equal quantities of warm water. A drench – for the non-farmer – is a liquid given directly into the mouth of the animal from a bottle which has usually a rubber or plastic end. This can be given twice a day until the appetite is restored when the mixture can be poured over the concentrated rations.

Younger or smaller animals require proportionately less. Heifers at bulling age need two fluid ounces once a day, weaned calves one fluid ounce a day and new-born calves two teaspoonsful each day.

TREATMENT OF MASTITIS

Both *Streptococcal* and *Staphylococcal mastitis* seem to be improved by cider vinegar although, as pointed out earlier in this section, the successful laboratory tests have been upon the more resistant *Streptococcus mammitis* not upon the antibiotic-sensitive *Staphylococcus agalactiae*.

The trouble with antibiotic treatment, apart from the cost, is the effect upon the milk because of the unacceptable residue of antibiotic formed therein.

Treatment with cider vinegar by means of a daily ration or drench of up to eight fluid ounces a day for three days, then half as much, usually produces clear, clot-free milk within seven days. A regular daily dose prevents further attacks. The milk can be sent to the dairy as soon as it is normal. Milk is never tainted nor harmed in any way from the use of cider vinegar.

When the shape or the texture of a quarter of the udder is badly affected it may take up to eight weeks to return to normal. However it has recently been reported that an injection of 5 mls. of cider vinegar directly into the infected quarter will reduce nodules and clear up infections almost immediately. Prevention and early treatment is best.

The treatment usually seems to work even when the infection is resistant to antibiotics. Some case histories illustrate this point.

Farmer W.J.E. of Haverfordwest learnt his skills from a cowman who came from the Cambridge University Farm who had always used cider vinegar for mastitis. He completely cured two of his cows and quite a few of his neighbour's which were still seriously ill even after massive doses of antibiotics from the veterinary surgeon.

Farmer J.C.O. of Axminster wrote that he had used it on his cattle for years, two tablespoonsful twice a day on their nuts. Before doing this they had terrible mastitis and warble fly.

Farmer R.J.I.W. who has a herd of Ayrshires in Cheshire used the Milk Marketing Board cell-count test to find sub-clinical mastitis. He had been using cider vinegar successfully for some time for clinical mastitis but was worried to find from the tests that a high incidence of invisible mastitis affected the untreated part of the herd. He then treated them all with cider vinegar. The first result was that many of the sub-clinical cases became clinical, but then all cleared up. He thought this might be a step in the elimination of the infection.

Farmer K.J.R. of the Isle of Wight after using cider vinegar on his forty-five Ayrshires for two years was able to say that mastitis had become a rare occurrence.

In the magazine *Dairy Farmer* for December 1967, Mike Walsh wrote how he had, like other readers, successfully used cider vinegar for mastitis but found his results to be not always consistent. He says it is useful in restoring a cow's appetite and also not expensive.

He goes on to mention that an eggcupful every morning will soon have any dairy farmer with rheumatism skipping around like a newborn lamb. And if the dairymaid has a slimming problem she will find it very useful although she will have to watch out for the rejuvenated dairy farmer!

A supplier of cider vinegar to Cumberland farmers relates how after a trial lasting just three weeks he thought cider vinegar wonderful stuff because it had completely cleared up a persistent mastitis problem. Furthermore, the cows had a bloom he had never ever experienced in the past.

MILK FEVER

Even when animals have a history of repeated severe attacks of milk fever, a daily four-ounce ration of cider vinegar given from six weeks before until three weeks after calving has been completely successful in preventing the condition.

ACETONAEMIA

This condition often arises from an unbalanced

diet. The liver normally, with the particular aid of certain carbohydrates, oxidizes fats. In acetonaemia it is unable to do this because of a shortage of these carbohydrates. The result is that various breakdown products of fat called *ketones* are released into the blood stream. Acetone is one of these and it causes a peculiar sweet smell of the breath and milk that is a characteristic of this disease, the other name for which is ketosis.

Glycerine and propylene glycol have both been recommended as treatments. Yet cider vinegar seems to provide an even better answer. It can be used as a preventive by giving two fluid ounces twice daily from three to six weeks before calving until four to six weeks after. As a treatment drench with eight fluid ounces of cider vinegar mixed with an equal quantity of warm water on the first day then two fluid ounces twice daily over feed for two to three weeks.

Mrs. E.M.C. of Calne, writing in *Farming Express*, said that her dairy herd had suffered from acetonaemia for many years. They tried both glycerine and potassium chlorate without satisfactory results even though they were expensive. She had read an article in the *Daily Express* discussing the properties of cider vinegar almost two years earlier and her family had used it ever since. She has seen her cows eat their cake within an hour of being drenched. She gives ¾-pint or ½-pint of cider vinegar according to animal size and there is rarely any loss of milk.

The paper's veterinary adviser thought that her results were a result of supplying the cow with the necessary organic acids which are normally present in ruminal fermentation.

IMPROVED MILK YIELDS AND CONDITION

Mrs. Marrable of Marle Green, Sussex, who has a herd of twenty milking Friesians and Short-horns, first tried small quantities of cider vinegar late in 1964. Here are her results for that and the succeeding two years:

	1964/65	1965/66	1966/67
Milk yield (lbs.)	10,085	10,509	11,507
Butterfat per cent.	3.61	3.59	3.56
Veterinary fees	£45	£15	£15

After the second year she wondered if other factors might have produced these changes, so she waited another year before feeling confirmed in her findings, which were published in *Farmer and Stockbreeder* in December 1967.

Mrs. Marrable showed the reporter how keen the cows were on the cider vinegar by tipping a small quantity on the grass when they gathered around to lick it up as eagerly as they would eat linseed cake.

This herd's fertility has improved and there have been no calving troubles or retained cleansings. The calves themselves appear extra vigorous and go to a local dealer who is prepared to pay slightly higher prices because of their sturdiness and good coats. All the

cattle on the farm have the supple skin and
shining coat so valued by stockmen.

Dr. Jarvis found even greater increase in milk
yields over a similar period, but his herd may
have been in a worse condition at the start than
Mrs. Marrable's.

DRYING OFF IN MILK COWS

Mastitis is common at this time, and as I have
indicated, cider vinegar is a valuable preventative. It has been suggested that drenching can
be avoided at this time if a very small ration of
concentrate, even as little as six cake nuts, is
placed by the cider vinegar ration in the
manger. Once this becomes an established
routine the cows often drink the vinegar from
their manger without any concentrate in addition. The period of preventative treatment
varies with the quality of hay or pasture
providing maintenance, and the milking poten-
tial, from between one and three weeks. It is
usual to give four fluid ounces a day for the
first week and then half as much for as long as
necessary.

FERTILITY

Users universally report improved fertility from
heifers and cows when they are on a four
fluid-ounce daily ration. This is particularly
striking in the high first service conception
rates in both bulling heifers and cows. Yet
other farmers do not find a regular dose so
effective as giving one pint of cider vinegar on

the concentrate just before serving.

Stock bulls on a regular four fluid-ounce daily ration tend to maintain semen of high fertility even during slack periods. The treatment also stimulates bulls who are uninterested.

I have previously referred to the report of Mrs. E.M.C. in *Farming Express*. She says that she gives cows half-a-pint before service and had all her cows and heifers in calf during the last winter. The vet said he was not certain of the action of cider vinegar on fertility, the possible explanation being the rich mineral properties of the vinegar, particularly the trace elements which may be of value in breeding efficiency.

No one seems to have tried this application on people — I wonder what would happen? Reports from research workers would be welcomed.

ARTHRITIS AND RHEUMATISM

Although not always successful it is well worth trying the two fluid ounces ration twice daily. Often when cattle are too stiff to get up or to graze properly the treatment is so effective that cows due to be culled for beef have recovered to complete several more lactations. In such cases it is important to give the cider vinegar regularly in order to prolong the productive life.

PIGS

Farrowing Fever

For prevention in susceptible sows, give them two fluid ounces a day for from two to three weeks prior and one to two weeks after farrowing. The piglets are usually more active and the sow does not lose her appetite. If she has farrowing fever then give two ounces daily for at least ten days.

Farmer G. Chatham of Kingsbridge found he was constantly having large veterinary bills because of farrowing fever. His losses of pigs and consequent debility were very bad. He used the two fluid ounces for two weeks before and one week after treatment and reported a marked improvement in his breeding stock. Since using cider vinegar he had no cases of farrowing fever or similar udder troubles. The young pigs were more lively and less laid on by sows. Since using cider vinegar he was of the opinion that both the quantity and quality of his pigs has greatly improved. He has asked that his experience be shared with other breeders to cut their losses by such a simple but safe treatment.

Scouring

As with calves, bacterial and nutritional scouring is often cured with cider vinegar in the drinking water of pigs.

Farmer K.J.R. of Newport, Isle of Wight had one pig which was scouring so badly it was almost dead. Ten days after the cider vinegar treatment was begun, the pig was back to normal.

Farmer D.F.W. of Chard has twenty-two breeding sows, some three years old. In the past he has had to have the vet two or three times to each at farrowing time. Now sometimes the vet comes once and sometimes not at all. He also is having better litters with nine to twelve reared. His vet's bill is down by two-thirds.

Incidentally, just before farrowing, he gives the sow either a pint of stout or one-and-a-half pints of rough cider and finds this makes them so docile that they lie down and farrow half asleep!

GOATS

In general, the treatments for goats are about half that for cattle.

Mr. J.L.R. of Colchester who has a herd of dairy goats, found cider vinegar particularly effective in the treatment of acetonaemia.

POULTRY

Turkeys and chickens have been reported to show an improved rate of growth when a teaspoonful of cider vinegar is added to each quart of drinking water.

Mr. John Woods of Preston, a poultry keeper on a considerable scale, made a controlled trial on birds in battery cages which had poor shell texture following respiratory infection. He added the cider vinegar at 1 per cent., that is two-and-a-half gallons per ton of feed. The addition was known to no-one but himself and his mill operative and he frankly said that he had little confidence of any beneficial results. He checked the shell texture at the end of two weeks with no apparent change. Almost as an afterthought, he checked again at the end of a month and found a most marked improvement. He assessed the number of cracked and porous eggs was reduced by 80 per cent. in the treated group.

HORSES AND PONIES

The suggested doses are three fluid ounces a day for small ponies, horses up to fifteen hands four fluid ounces, and over fifteen hands six ounces per day. As many horses are rather conservative in their eating habits it is best to give it with their favourite food. Drenching is not recommended for horses or ponies with cider vinegar or with other fluids for that matter, unless it is done by the veterinary surgeon, as the procedure can lead to respiratory complications.

LOST APPETITE

A ration that is high in concentrates frequently causes horses and ponies to become bored, when they lose interest in their food. The use of cider vinegar on the feed often stimulates the appetite as well as improving the general condition.

DUNG EATING

This rather unpleasant habit is clearly discouraged by the rapid removal of the dung. It could be, however, that it has a nutritional origin because a course of cider vinegar, which is rich in minerals, often cures the condition.

COAT CONDITION

Horses and ponies improve the suppleness and bloom of their coat when on a course of cider vinegar in a significant number of instances.

POISONING

Because of the effect that cider vinegar has both in improving the appetite and in restoring the intestinal organisms that are so often altered or destroyed either by accidentally-eaten poisons or veterinary treatment with a similar effect — for example, antibiotics often damage the bacteria essential to good health even though they may be necessary for treatment — there will be gradual but helpful assistance from the use of cider vinegar in such circumstances, when used in addition to the usual procedures.

EQUINE INFLUENZA AND COUGH

I have noted only one communication upon this subject, but very interesting.

Lord C. from Dorset writes that he has been feeding cider vinegar to horses for a number of years and although they have mixed freely with sufferers from cough or equine flu, they have so far been immune. Perhaps this is a result of the cider vinegar treatment.

SHEEP

Twin Lamb Disease

This is a toxaemia of pregnancy which usually occurs in ewes in the fourth and fifth months of pregnancy, often when they are carrying two or three lambs. When contracted, it is frequently fatal so prevention is important. The incidence has been said to reduce when two fluid ounces a day of cider vinegar are sprinkled over the concentrate. Treatment is certainly worth trying by using a drench with quarter-of-a-pint of cider vinegar and an equal amount of warm water and then the two ounces a day for one or two weeks.

INDEX